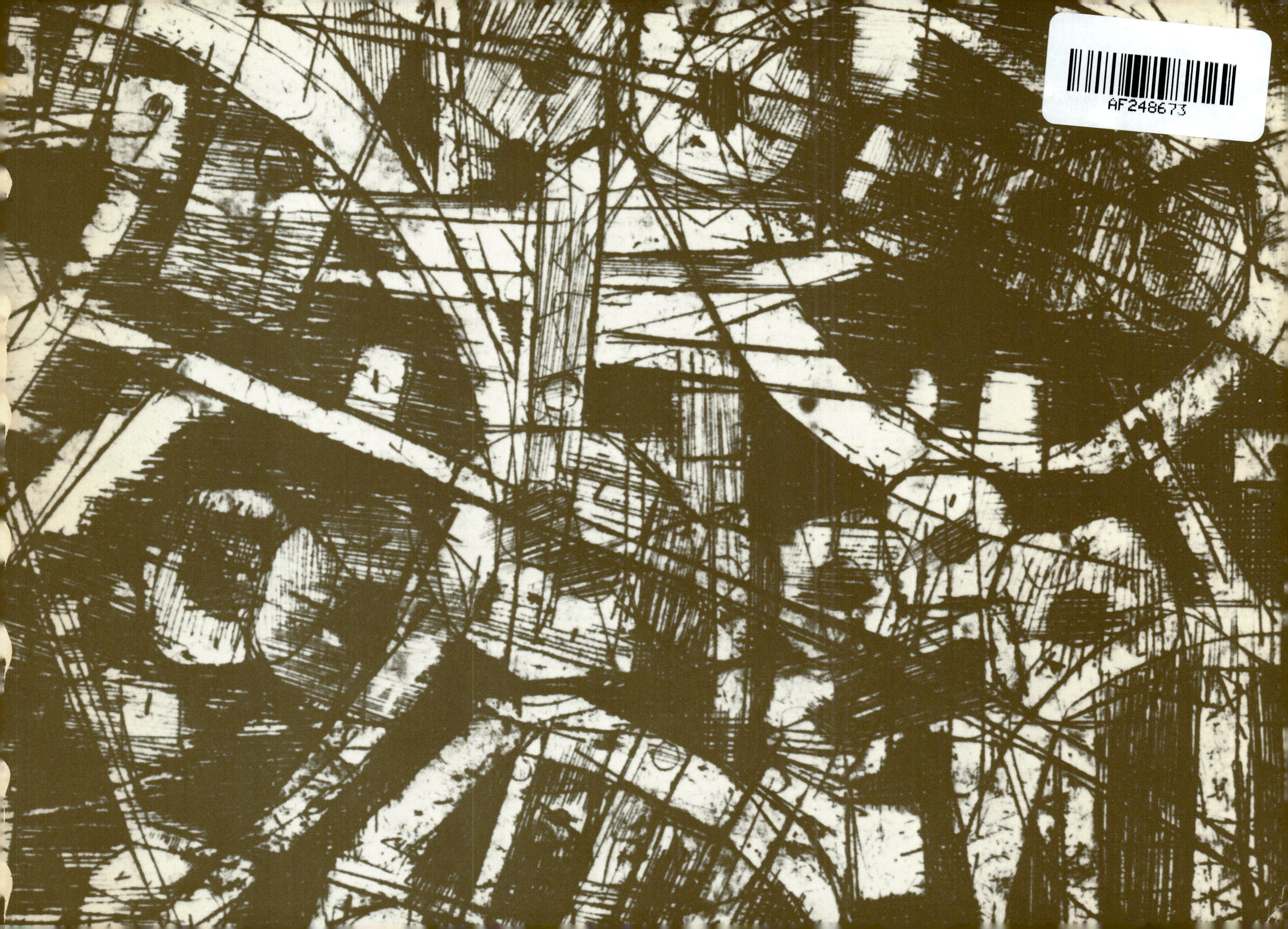

# Contemporary Australian Printmakers 1

Exhibition assembled by the

## Print Council of Australia

with the co-operation of the
Department of Foreign Affairs, Canberra

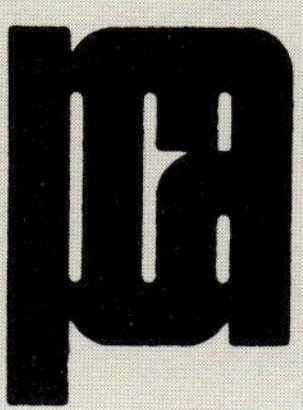


| | |
|---|---|
| Publisher | Print Council of Australia |
| Foreword | Alison French, Lecturer in Fine Arts, Melbourne State College, Victoria |
| Editor | Lilian Wood, Editor, Directory of Australian Printmakers 1976 |
| Design | David Sampietro |
| Photography | Edwin Burchett |
| Printing and Typesetting | Gardner Printing Co. (Vic.) Pty. Ltd. |

Personal photographs provided by individual artists

The assistance of Qantas Airways in the transport of this exhibition is gratefully acknowledged.

National Library of Australia
**ISBN 0 909227 05 5**

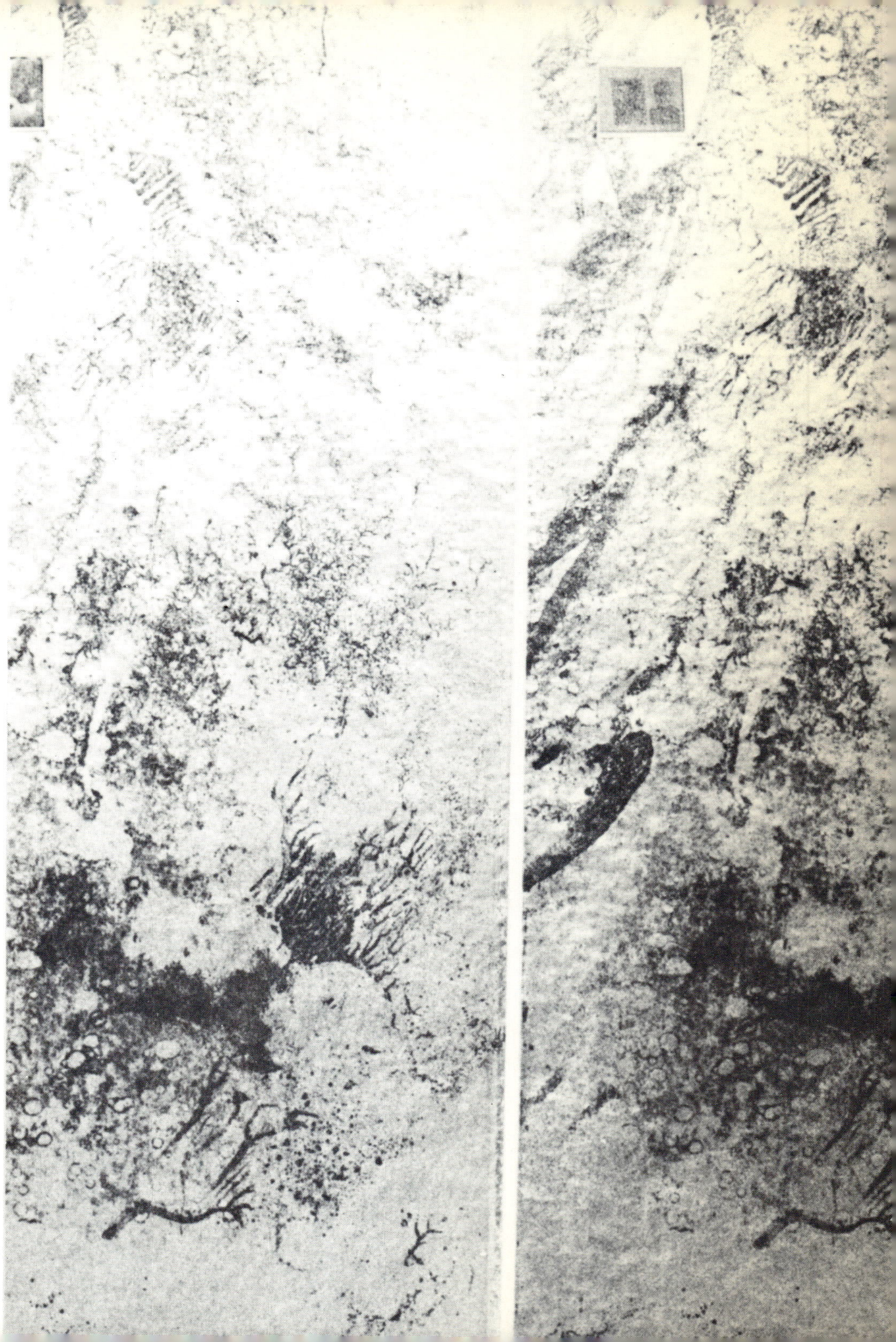

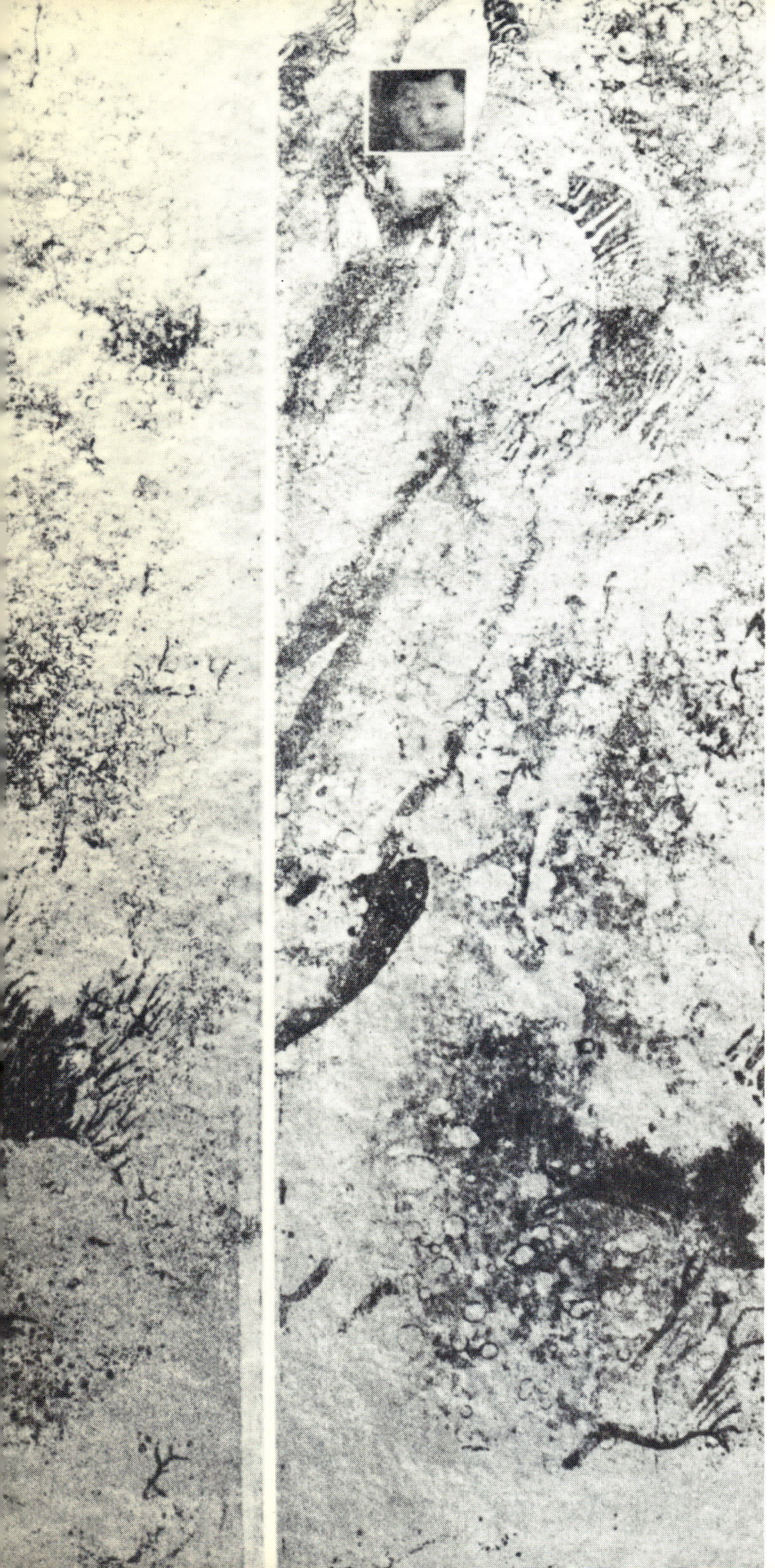

The **Print Council of Australia** acknowledges with gratitude the generous support of the Department of Foreign Affairs, Canberra, and the co-operation of Australian diplomatic posts in the US which have enabled this exhibition to be shown in major North American and Canadian venues.

The first venue in the exhibition itinerary for **Contemporary Australian Printmakers 1** is Bell Gallery, Brown University, Providence, Rhode Island, USA, whose Director, Ms Nancy Versaci, has been instrumental in initiating this project in conjunction with members of staff of the School of Art, The Victorian College of the Arts, Australia.

Established in 1966, the Print Council of Australia consists of artists, organisations, schools and interested people who consider that achievement of the aims of the Council will make a significant contribution to art in Australia.

The chief aim of the Print Council of Australia is to promote the production and appreciation of hand printed graphics in Australia. Since 1967, print exhibitions have been assembled each year for showing in State and regional galleries throughout Australia; exhibitions of Australian graphics have been sent to USA, Europe and South-East Asia.

Exhibitions of work by students under instruction at art schools in all Australian States have also figured largely in Council annual activities.

The Council's publication Imprint, dealing with various aspects of printmaking and collecting is circulated to members, libraries, institutions and is available in State gallery bookshops.

Information concerning print exhibitions and competitions within Australia and overseas is sought and circulated among printmakers.

Selections from limited print editions commissioned by the Council are made available to members annually.

These activities are made possible by the work of a voluntary committee supported by membership funds, donations, the assistance of a grant from the Visual Arts Board of the Australia Council, and the support of all Australian State Governments. The society's programme is administered with the assistance of an executive officer from offices situated at 105 Collins Street. Melbourne 3000. (STD 03) 654 2460.

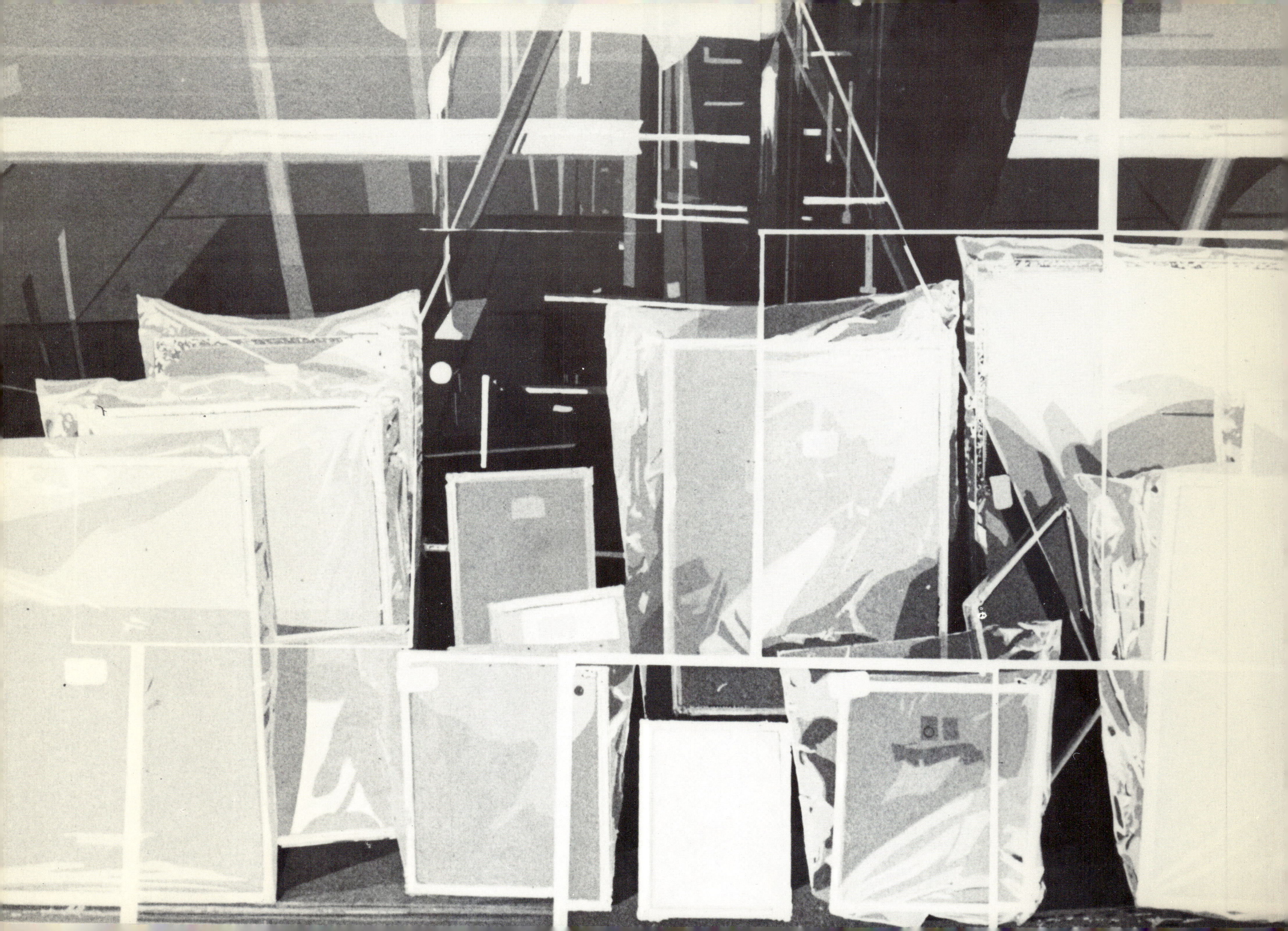

# Contemporary Australian Printmakers I

Presented by the Print Council of Australia in conjunction with the
Department of Foreign Affairs, Canberra, this exhibition has been
assembled from recent work of thirty-five artists. It was not selected with
the intention of providing an exhaustive survey of trends in contemporary
printmaking throughout Australia: the range and number of works do not
make judgements along these lines appropriate. Rather, this exhibition gives
the viewer an opportunity of seeing some recent aspects of Australian
printmaking. To a certain extent a survey of the past two decades is also
evident. Those who did so much to establish printmaking in the early 1960s
are represented by recent work (Ruth Faerber, Robert Grieve, Grahame
King, Earle Backen) while a newer generation is seen in the prints of Greg
Moncrieff, Sally Robinson, Helen Taylor, Stephen Spurrier, Allan Mitelman,
and Ray Arnold. Before considering the range of imagery and styles in
individual works, some general comments on developments in Australian
printmaking might provide a useful framework for the viewer.

**Margaret Preston (1875-1963)**
Black Cockatoos
Woodcut
Image size : 25 x 25 cm
Edition 25

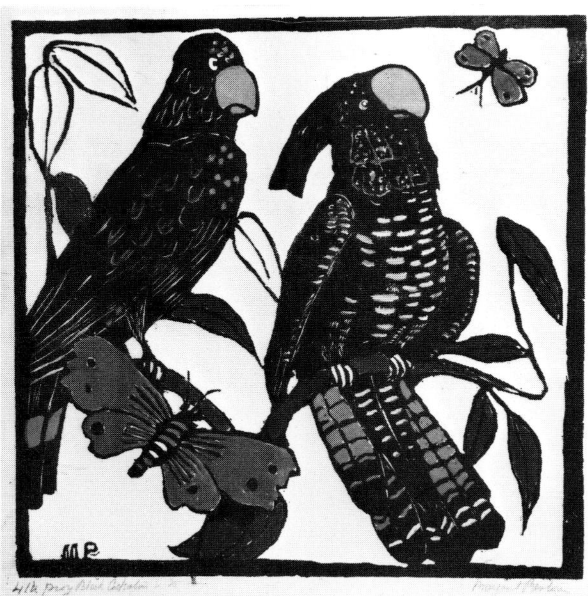

*Reproduced: A Survey of Australian Relief Prints*
            *1900/1950, Deutsher Galleries,*
            *1978, plate*

**Lionel Lindsay (1874-1961)**
The Dancer
Etching and aquatint
Image size : 18.5 x 14.5 cm
Edition 50

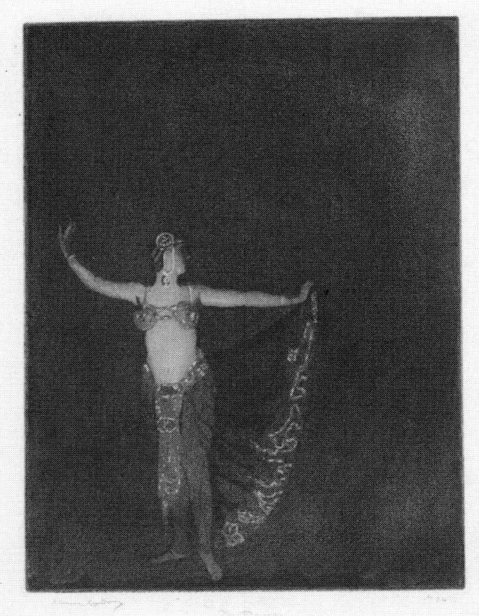

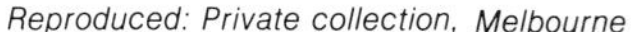

*Reproduced: Private collection, Melbourne*

**John Shirlow (1869-1936)**
View of Melbourne, the River
Etching
Image size : 28 x 65 cm
Edition

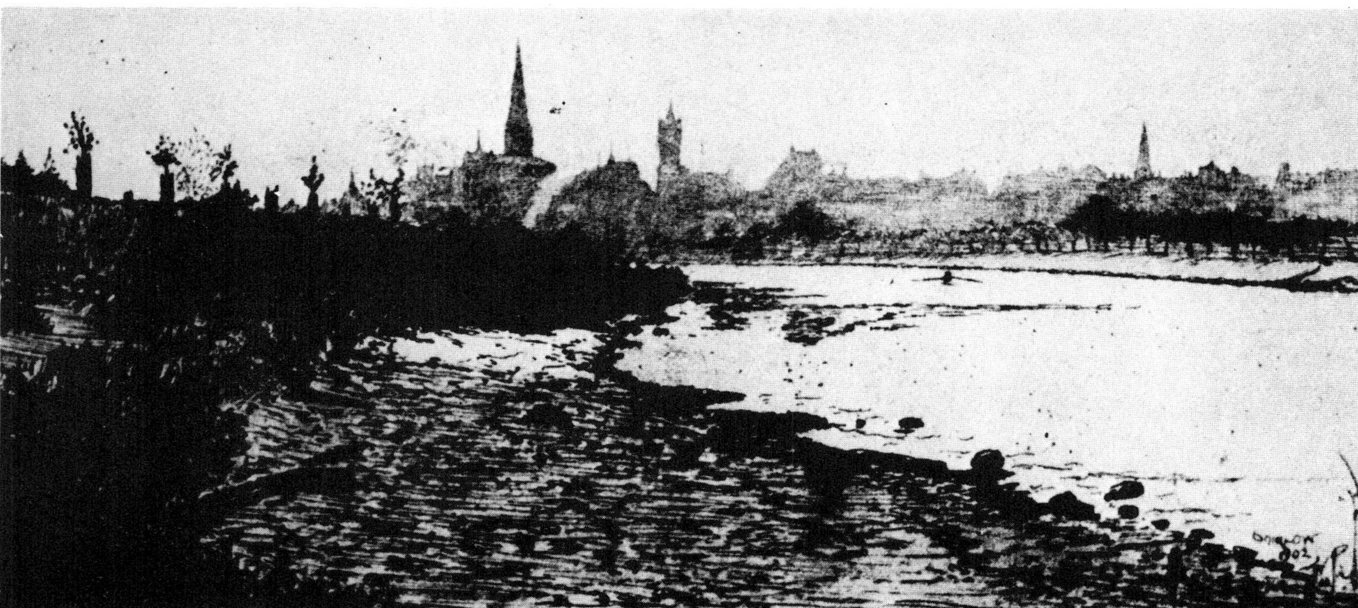

*Reproduced: Imprint No. 3/1977*

# The Context of Contemporary Australian Printmaking

The first comprehensive historical survey of printmaking in Australia[1] made it clear that there is a lack of internal continuity in the Australian printmaking tradition. The purposes, styles and concerns of the modern work have very little in common with the earliest topographical engravings — illustrations for successive voyages to the South Seas and albums describing the progress of civilisation in alien lands.

Until recently the history of printmaking in Australia has not closely paralleled the history of Australian painting. Creative activity in Australian printmaking first occurred in the first two decades of the twentieth century; the second phase began to emerge in the 1950s and gained full momentum in the 1960s.

In the nineteenth century, printmaking largely remained tied to the illustrative vein and was not a medium for serious and independent creative activity when the ground-swell of nationalist sentiment in the late 1880s and '90s was producing some of the most vital and original images in Australian landscape. These were impressionistic images in which the dried-out textures of the bush might fill the frame, or the slim straggly strokes of a gum tree pierce a horizon line, vibrating as the blonde tonalities of the land met the harsh blues of the summer sky. These qualities were not found in the vast panoramas or romantic vistas which satisfied the European taste for the picturesque.

Printmaking was very popular in the first half of the twentieth century, but the only printmaker regarded as having made a significant contribution to Australian art in other media is Margaret Preston, whose vibrantly coloured wood and linocuts of still lifes and Aboriginal motifs introduced a simplicity of form and a vigorous decorativeness in crisp contrast to an art scene otherwise characterised by the endless repetition of gum trees. This period also saw a predominantly etching tradition established by such artists as John Shirlow and Lionel Lindsay, a tradition which was to fade and be swept away when the economic depression of the 1930s decimated art societies and dispersed artists.

In the immediate post-World War II period, prints were occasionally included in mixed exhibitions with drawings and watercolours; imported print exhibitions were rare. For artists wishing to explore printmaking, access to specialized materials and equipment was dauntingly difficult and no organized instruction courses were available, a situation which had to wait upon the arrival of migrant artist-teachers trained in the main streams of German, English or to a lesser extent, French traditions — Udo Sellbach, Tate Adams, and Karin Schepers. The return of Australian artists from overseas to work and teach also stimulated the regeneration of printmaking

activity in the 1960s.[2] Of this latter group, work from Grahame King, Earle Backen, Robert Grieve, Murray Walker and David Rose appears in this exhibition.

Barbara Hanrahan's description of a graphics studio established at the South Australian School of Art, North Adelaide in February 1960 reveals some of the anomalies art students experienced at that time:

> When I think back to that period, the marvellous ritual of printmaking — the queer stink of meths and turps, the mysteries of acid and resin — is linked with all the outdated, inconvenient beauty of the old building: its fantastic creeper-swathed facade; Venus and David in the Drawing Room; the Clay Modelling room in the basement with its alarming assortment of outsize eyes and noses. It was 1960 — modern times, and Jackson Pollock was Hero, but the last vestiges of an era of repoussé and artistic anatomy lingered on.[3]

By 1963 enough had been produced for a major survey of Australian prints[4] to be assembled and toured by the Art Gallery of New South Wales. In 1966 the Print Council of Australia was founded. The period between its first touring exhibition (1967) and the present has seen a proliferation of printmaking courses and the establishment of specialist print galleries and workshops.[5]

In addition to important collections in major State galleries, good print holdings are being built in regional centres; positions offered by universities and colleges for Artists-in-Residence have helped broaden financial support for printmakers. In contrast with the past, printmaking is now more centrally placed in the Australian art scene.

Most printmakers in this exhibition work in a variety of media: Jock Clutterbuck is a sculptor; John Coburn produces murals and designs tapestries (his curtains for the Sydney Opera House are probably his best-known commission). Major painters like Fred Williams and Roger Kemp have equal reputations for their prints and regard their activities in each medium as independently significant. The majority live and work in Sydney and Melbourne on the eastern seaboard where printmaking facilities and instruction developed earlier than elsewhere. Adelaide, which has maintained a similar printmaking tradition, is represented by Barbara Hanrahan and Ann Newmarch. The west coast artists are here represented by Ray Beattie and Helen Taylor in Perth, and developments there in recent years are producing a lively group whose contribution to Australian

printmaking could be expected to increase.[6]
A problem of survey exhibitions is that their inevitable selectiveness, rather than allowing critics to discuss individual talents, encourages them to talk of general trends and influences, both environmental and artistic. Conclusions of this nature should be drawn only after viewing many such shows in the context of one-man exhibitions.

In the early 1960s rather narrow observations were being made on the basis of partial exposures of Australian painting in London. They reveal the dangers of attempting to search for the uniquely different Australian image. Such an approach would be equally inappropriate in viewing the present exhibition.

As printmaking was beginning to re-emerge in Australia, a spate of one-man and group exhibitions of Australian painting was flooding the London galleries. In a blandly international art scene, proponents of regional and exotic realism seemed determined to preserve ''the image of Australia as a cratered terrain peopled by myth-haunted heroes.''[7]

Critics concerned with discovering an ''Australian image'' cultivated and exaggerated the myth of isolation because it seemed to indicate a unique phenomenon: hence *The Tatler* comment ''There surely is the exhilaration of starting from scratch.''[8]

But Australian painting at that time was based on the consolidation of European experiences. Those who gained success in London did so by living there. Paintings which slotted into the ''Australian image'' being created by the critics were only a small, if exotic, aspect of these exhibitions, and from the mid-1960s onwards international trends of hard-edge abstraction, junk art, optical art and pop art were starting to dominate.

By the time of the major historical survey exhibition of Australian Art at the Tate Gallery in 1963, Robert Melville admitted:

> We are far too anxious to see the Australians make a
> unique contribution to painting... They think we want
> them to specialize in quaint and uncouth scenes from
> Australia's past, as a light relief to the great and
> serious abstract art of Europe and America.[9]

The belief that the Australian school ''needs to be studied as we study Oriental, Mexican and African art before it can be enjoyed''[10] as Eric Newton advised in 1961, is certainly misguided now, as it was even then. Australian art, and Australian printmaking in particular, is embedded in a European context.

This is particularly so in view of the influences that have served to foster and mould Australian printmaking — especially the contribution of migrant artists and overseas training. It would seem that Brian Seidel's observation, made in 1965, remains relevant today:

> Australian printmakers remain, so far, within the
> International style following a line concurrent with that
> of Europe and the USA and having direct affinity.[11]

An obsession with an Australian identity or nationalist images (which has recurred at specific times in the history of Australian painting) is neither apparent in, nor relevant to, contemporary Australian printmaking. A more appropriate response to an exhibition of this kind is to look at the imagery presented, rather than seek to place the works within environmental trends.

**Fred Williams,** who has produced one of the most substantial bodies of graphic work in Australia, mainly in the field of etching, is represented here by two recent lithographs. This medium seems to correspond with interests in concurrent paintings, where a strong black fluid line is often reintroduced to bind the fluidly tactile and dense forms of motifs such as the Werribee Gorge. This is a development away from the sparser imagery of his earlier paintings and etchings in which elements of the landscape were reduced to tiny marks and squiggles. These were dispersed with seeming randomness across an open composition that simultaneously confronts the viewer with the macrocosm of an aerial view and the microcosm of the fragmented textures of the land itself.

Fred Williams' alternative to the impressionistic pastoral images of the turn of the nineteenth century and the burnt, eroded visions of Russell Drysdale in the 1940s and 50s, is widely acknowledged as having taught a new generation to see their landscape anew. Yet he claims that he never thought of himself as a landscape painter. Asked if he sees himself as making a statement about the Australian landscape, he stresses his interest in painterly concerns, rather than national myth making, and comments on one of his works:

> Here I consider I've got to the essence. That is how a
> landscape should be, even if it isn't. It doesn't refer to
> any particular country any longer. You are only
> conscious of those little marks.[12]

One younger exhibitor, **Sally Robinson,** depicts camels that have none of the ethereal mystery of the small pale creatures that extend from the loins of the lone explorers Burke and Wills in Sidney Nolan's paintings of their ill-

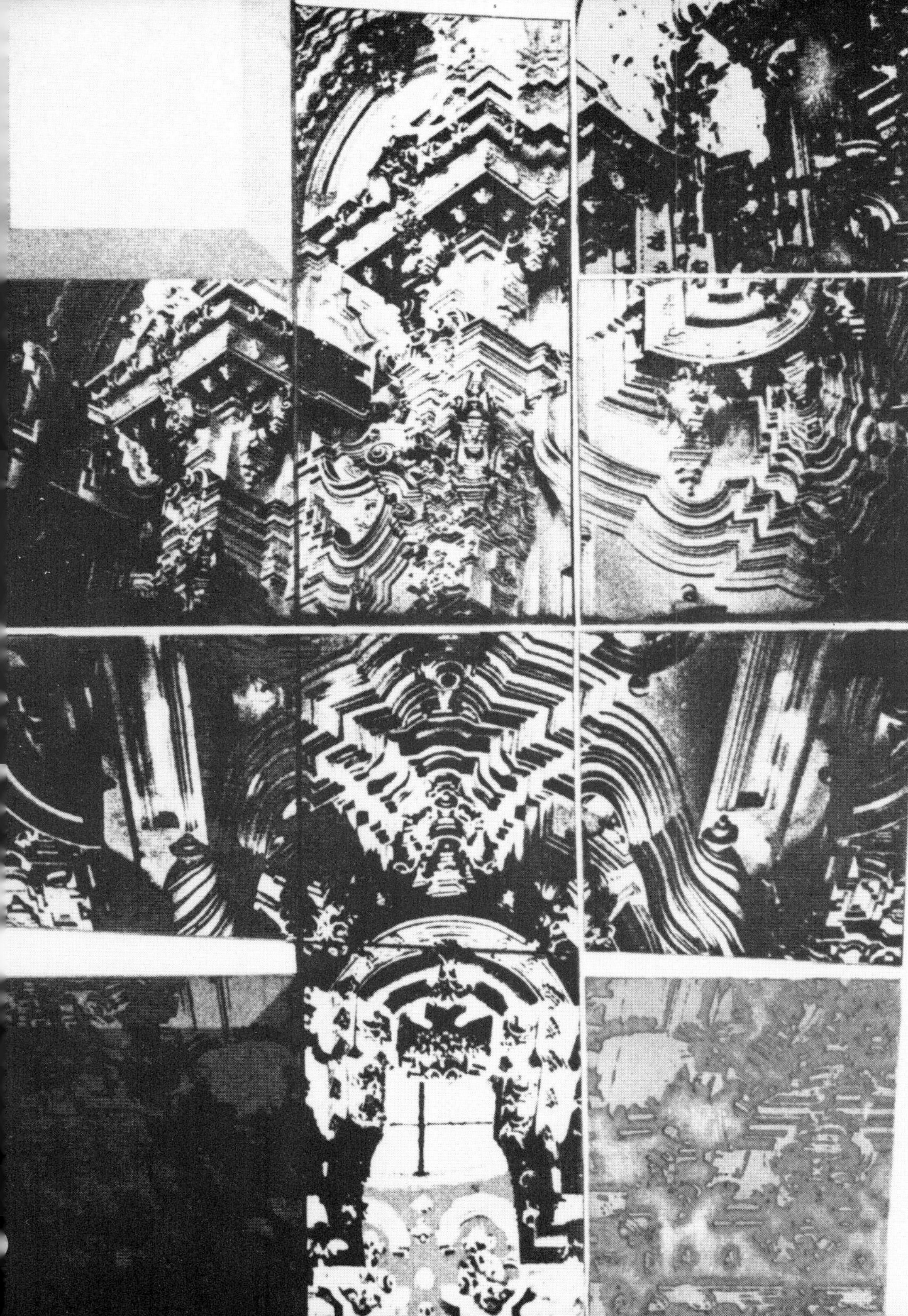

fated expedition. In her brightly coloured photographic silkscreen image of *Central Australia* she simply confronts us with two rather arrogant, slightly vulgar personages.

To conclude these introductory comments about the context of contemporary printmaking in Australia the following points should be reiterated. There has been a lack of continuity in printmaking in Australia. Developments have not always paralleled those in Australian art generally: in different ways both have remained embedded in an international context. Finally, images of national identity are not the key to contemporary Australian printmaking.

# Some Aspects of Image Making in Contemporary Australian Printmaking

The only real things in this world are ideas; objects are nothing but the revealers of the appearances of ideas, and by consequence have importance only as signs of ideas.[12]

### Printmaking: Personal Vision and Processes of Objectification

The above quotation provided a source for insights into the image making of the rather diffuse range of concerns evident in the contemporary prints exhibited in this show.

In a very basic sense in the context of two dimensional imagery, the print, being relatively small scale, and having possibilities for textural surfaces and contrast between line, mark and paper, also has the most right to assume the qualities of an object. The printmaking process itself is essentially an objectifying one, as various stages of technique and intuitive projection are necessary to convert an image from the mind to a plate (or series of plates in the case of a colour print), then to sheets of blank paper. This technique thus simultaneously transposes, modifies and creates ideas in separate steps. The printed image, like an object, is the product of construction.

Some techniques do allow for the illusion of a more spontaneous image: in lithography, for example, the image is drawn, transferred or photographically processed onto the stone or plate in lithographic crayon or ink. This allows considerable initial freedom. The sweeping brushstrokes of Grahame King's *East Wind* provide a clear example of the possibilities for lithography to create a loose, flowing image.

Screenprinting (serigraphy, silkscreen) is a process which requires less complicated equipment, and has recently become popular in Australia. It is also very much suited to a direct approach. Barbara Hanrahan's decoratively naive figures are simply drawn onto the screen, but most of the printmakers in this exhibition who employ screenprinting as their medium combine both photographic and drawn images to different effects. Greg Moncrieff juxtaposes the two worlds, Jan Senbergs fuses them, while Sally Robinson and Ann Newmarch allow overlays of colour to alter our response to the photographic records of their experience.

In contrast to these two surface methods of printing, intaglio printing methods, which are most evident in this exhibition, involve more complicated stages of image making and are the most objectifying processes. The quality and depth of the line are controlled by acids and etching time, as is the tonal range from subtle greys to deep blacks. Very fine and sensitive line is possible; the idiosyncratic pressure of an individual hand is delicately recorded. A comparison of the different qualities of line in works by Ray Beattie, Petr Herel, Murray Walker and Helen Taylor bears out the infinite possibilities of this medium.

Mezzotint is another form of intaglio printing which is only recently being re-explored for creative, as opposed to purely reprographic, purposes. In **Graeme Peebles'** prints, the densities of texture and the illusion of soft surfaces made possible by this technique, infuse an odd sense of reality into the extreme formality of the design. In *Schaedenfreude* the blind softly peering chickens with claws sprouting upwards like flowers hang tied from a crossbar. The precision in the drawing of the knotted string which holds them there contrasts with the soft vulnerability of rotting flesh, the grey of the bird and the dense matt black background. The illusion of reality conveyed by the medium is strangely at odds with the peculiar selectivity and subjectivity of the vision.

### Isolating the Object

These prints are among several in the exhibition in which attention is closely focussed on objects — invariably objects of the artists' own domestic or creative environment. Geoff La Gerche's paint brushes and jars, William Kelly's nude models arrayed across the grid of the studio floor, Normana Wight's crochet jackets and Helen Taylor's discreet interiors also assert to a greater or lesser extent an aura of the physical world as known and touched, no matter how much their curious isolation in each particular image might cause one to question assumed attitudes towards these objects. However in Bea Maddock's confrontations of couples kissing, the event becomes the object. In these images any search for ideas that can be expressed in terms of abstractions remains extremely elusive and if these objects are to be seen as "revealers of the appearances of ideas", as suggested in the initial quotation, it is clear that the ideas cannot be extrapolated from their "appearances". For these artists the "appearances" have a fascination in their own right; the interest is much more in the sign than the idea. The interest in these works therefore lies in the selection, isolation and manipulation of the object — the creation of the image.

In the case of **Normana Wight,** whose earlier work was hard-edged abstraction, the more painterly application of vibrant primary colour over photographic image means that the crochet jacket — isolated arms outstretched in the white blankness of the page — retains its presence as part of the mundane everyday world with a naive sense of personality, a reminder that it is to be worn; at the same time it becomes a decorative object.

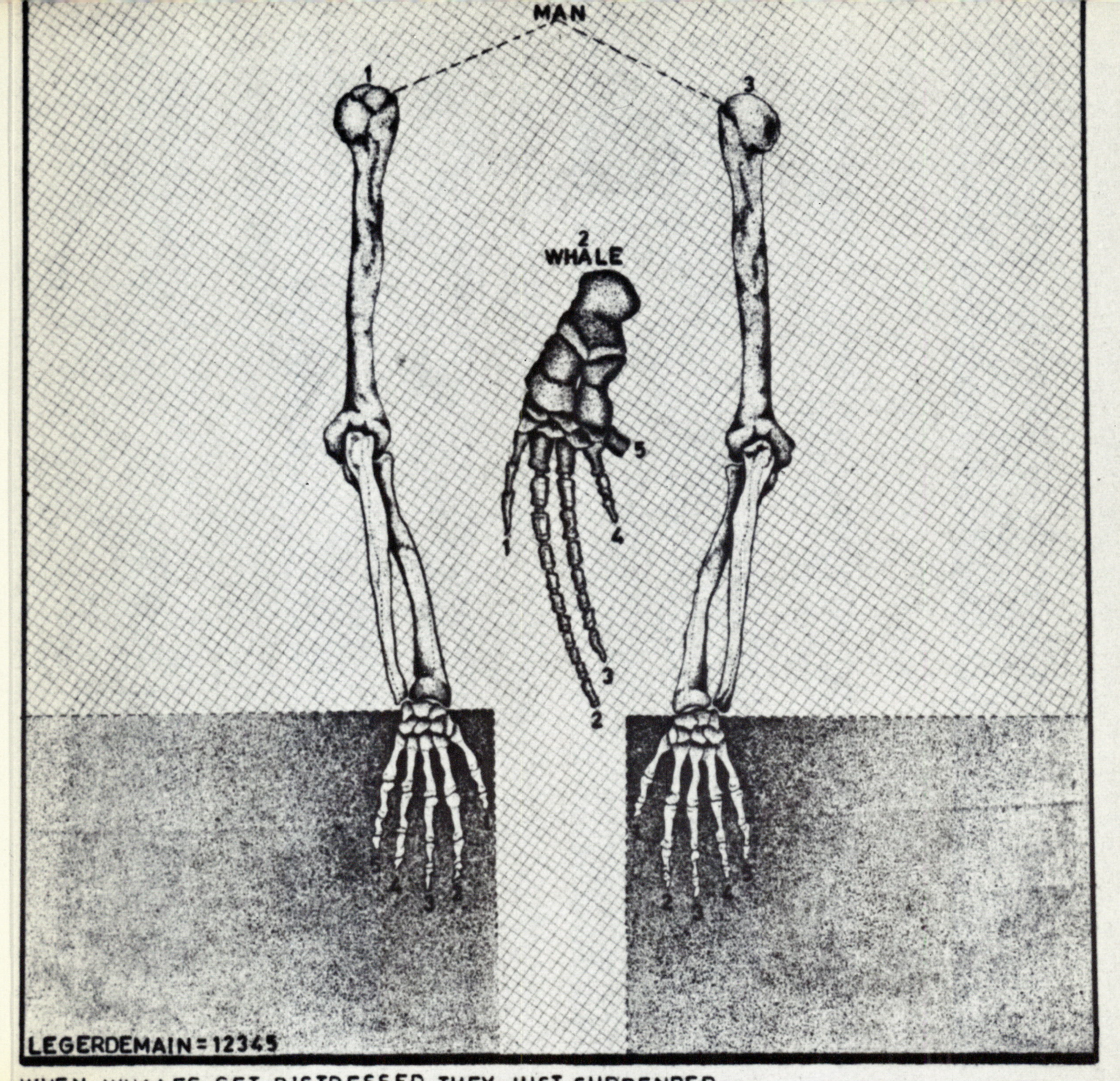

MAN
WHALE
LEGERDEMAIN = 12345
WHEN WHALES GET DISTRESSED THEY JUST SURRENDER.

**Helen Taylor** provides an environment for her objects and seems to be equally interested in both. Her awareness of their formal decorative qualities isolates them from a norm of domestic casualness, as seen in the frozen quality of the tissues bursting from their floral packet. The capacity of the etching technique to stress the individuality of the drawn line counters the seeming neutrality of the image, while the selectivity of Taylor's vision intensifies our perception of each item as an individual object.

For **Geoff La Gerche,** whose reputation exists mainly as a painter, the etching process makes possible the beautiful textures and scrubby effects of hairy brush ends. These and the highlights of reflections on glass jars have as much a painterly effect as an illusionary one. The vision is even more highly selective than Taylor's. Close focus on objects, their scale and the purposeful neutrality of background refuses to provide the viewer with a naturalistic context that might impinge upon them. In *Nine Brushes,* surely one of the most beautiful prints of the exhibition, objects are animated. There is a strong sense of the individuality of each brush, mysteriously suspended in space. Their subtle alignments and groupings establish a gentle flow which rises in slight sweeps from left to right through the long horizontal format, catching them up in a scarcely obtrusive dance across the page.

## Objectifying the Image

Image-making is a process of objectification for both **William Kelly** and **Bea Maddock.** For all the attempted naturalism of the human figure, any interest in its personal aura is negated by the neutral facial expression, and by the reductive focus upon the body against a formal referent, invariably a grid. The birdseye perspective forces the viewer to perceive the displacement of each limb as another geometric dynamic parallel to the picture plane. In this context the severe foreshortening of the left leg in *Person on Studio Floor (Male)* would seem to remind one less of a naturalistic sprawl than of the potential of a vertical form to rise into our space at right angles to the picture plane. The diagonal hatching of the shadows sets up a potentially circular swing of the bodies through the diagonal axis of the composition and reinforces Kelly's perennial concern for his forms to be viewed from any point, a dynamic which he invites by placing each component of his inscriptions at each corner of the composition.

Kelly is concerned to objectify the figure in the most extreme sense of the word in both his prints and paintings, which always follow the same format. Maddock also objectifies events, but in her prints the human element is never denied. It is simultaneously registered and transformed. These two etchings were originally part of a set of four in which the human action of the kiss is explored in different relationships. In each print a photographic source has been transferred to the plate. As the scale of the blowup varies so does the size and density of the dots, which establish the tonal variation

and set up a fine grid. In *Four By Two IV* it is as if the elderly couple are being viewed from a distance through a fine mesh screen. Their confrontation is distanced, neutralised by this and by the large patches of shadow and sunlight flooding across the faces, which leeches the couple of identity and heightens a sense of their fusion. For example, detail of the man's ear is faintly, but oddly recognised and can also be seen simply as a wrinkled soft shape. In the midst of this dissolution of matter, a formal structure is retained around intersecting diagonals which repeat the infra-structure of the diagonal grid of dots. This establishes an odd sense of a rocking symmetry that locks the couple firmly in an image that epitomises mutuality. The curve of their cheeks echo each other; as he moves over her there is a sense of progressive dissolution almost as if she were another stage of his person.

In *Four By Two I* the relationship is vibrantly dynamic. An excited energy is generated in the intensity of contact — mouth pursed, eyes in shadow, the kiss is planted on the grinning face of the boy. In this image, which overall has a much darker tonality and more heightened contrasts, the thickness of printing in the blacker areas has a velvet depth and yet there is also an odd scratchy feeling because of the closeness of the dots. These effects would not be possible in the blander surface of photographic silkscreen printing, a technique which Bea Maddock also practices widely to achieve different sorts of imagery. Here, in the context of the black dots, the light tones have a pin-pointing, bursting, vibrating quality, and so an explosion of energies that is the essence of the original photograph resonates through the etching.

The repetition of numbers printed beneath the photographic image directs the viewer to the status of each print as part of a series, yet it is itself an important part of a composite image containing both, by its proximity and by its tendency to establish perspectives for viewing the image. The direction of the numbers sets up a circular rhythm for viewing the heads. The softness of tone in each square, varying in density, also echoes the pulsating rhythm of the dots, and the clean sharp cross formation establishes a grid system, yet another pattern for viewing the composition of the forms.

In this way event becomes object, but never at the expense of the event. The human element is simultaneously registered and transformed.

## A Wider Reference: Social Themes and Personal Vision

In contrast to those printmakers concerned with a close focus on an external world, selecting, isolating and manipulating objects — such as Kelly, La Gerche, Peebles, Maddock, Wight and Helen Taylor — there are those who encompass a wider social context. In many cases their method is screenprinting, and the source of their imagery the public media or private photographs. In the case of Latimer, Moncrieff and Hanrahan, statements are derived from the juxtaposition of images drawn from public, social or institutional myths, and yet the attitudes they display towards these concerns are not programmatic. They project a personal vision in a very different way from the more neutral presentations of Sally Robinson and Ann Newmarch, whose imagery is derived from and tied very directly to records of personal experience. In the case of both these artists it is the use of colour which directs the viewer's response to the image. Aspects of the individual's everyday activities are reproduced and seen as legitimate subjects, no matter how mundane or commonplace: recall Wight's crochet jacket, previously discussed.

**Ann Newmarch,** whose works project a feminist stance, often explores sex roles and the exploitation of women by the mass media, and she has produced explicitly didactic works such as political posters.[13] The works by Ann Newmarch in this exhibition are much less dogmatic and more personal but not in a limited, private sense.

In the screenprint *Peggy* the woman's capable activities in a man's world might be seen as a celebration of Women's Liberation, but the impact of the image seems to centre around idiosyncracies of the woman's personality and dress: her personal vulnerabilities and her strengths are candidly revealed in a photo that has the private feel of a family snapshot. This imbues the image with an aura of personal authenticity. The scale of the image and the mauve and pink colouration, together with the choice of blue for the label, clearly play upon clichés of sex-typing. But our prime interest in the image is in Peggy herself, and not in any abstractions which she might stand for. Peggy resists typecasting in either cliché — whether as passivity trapped in a female body that can only draw attention to itself in order to manipulate men, or as the "liberated woman". Because this is so, the ambiguities and the reality of these clichéd abstractions are actually most fully realised.

**Barbara Hanrahan** has always been a strong individualist. Her personal vision, expressed in a distinctive idiosyncratic style, has remained consistent despite passing trends and fashions. Of all the printmakers in this exhibition, her style, with its use of dominant black outline to contain colour, owes the most to the possibilities of the woodcut medium. This influence has been transferred to the silkscreen. It is not surprising that she greatly admires the work of Margaret Preston,[14] whose significance to printmaking in Australia in the 1920s and 30s was mentioned in the first part of this essay. Thus some aspects of a rare continuity between printmaking of that period and today can be seen in her work. The fact that the direct and simple techniques of wood and linocut do not appear in this exhibition, and indeed are not used widely in Australia today, might be due to the desire of contemporary Australian printmakers to explore the more varied possibilities of new and more complex technologies. An example is the recent popularity of photographic images which can be reproduced through lithographic, etching and screenprinting processes.

In contrast to more sophisticated references to the external social world produced by the photographic image, Barbara Hanrahan's drawings have a childlike naivety. The subject matter, however, is far from childlike and a wry wit sharpens, yet also counters, bitterness. She claims that she doesn't "want to produce propaganda", but to produce prints that are "sensitive and personal". The fact that she prefers to draw each colour separation herself rather than have a master technician transform a single painting into a print by photographic colour separation, reveals a certain dissatisfaction with technology.

Her imagery has always centred on women. From her early work onwards a recurring theme has been a private mythology of grotesquely patterned Earth mothers. Images of Adam and Eve also recur as do references to the Garden of Eden. In *Wedding Night* the flowers on the fringed rugs and the pillows recall these previous references and seem to function as a reminder of an archetypal paradise soon to be lost. In *Men and Women* she uses a device common to many of her prints: the division of the image into separate, yet simultaneous experience. The men, blank eyed and coolly disengaged, are formally lined up in a row on the bottom of the page with their suits and ties, whilst above them pink, orange and mauve ladies float on a black ground, vulnerably exposed, their sexual histories and preferences labelled, or revealed in their individual stances and expressions. Hanrahan has commented on her interest in the dichotomy of reality and dreams and the theme of dissociation from the every day world. The depiction of each woman conveys with wit and pathos the internal inconsistencies and tensions in their awareness of their own desires and of the roles they must adopt in order to obtain them. The X-ray technique simultaneously reveals for us the women's sense of themselves and how they read the expectations crowding behind blank stares of the clothed men. The cry to a father paradoxically casts the row of men in another role. The foetuses within the women's wombs become more than a simple indication of their sexual history: they allude to a new generation which will perpetuate the cycle of alienation.

> Do not mind my crying Papa, I am not crying for pain,
> Do not mind my shaking Papa, I am not shaking for
> fear.
> Though the wind is hideous to hear,
> And I see the snow and the rain,
> When will you come back again Papa, Papa?
> Do not mind my crying Papa, I am not crying for pain.

Barbara Hanrahan's interest in the relationship of men and women is clearly set in a much broader context than the immediacies of specific sexual exploitations of particular societies. This, plus her fascination with decorative detail, naive directness of vision and "primitive" style, lifts the imagery above propaganda.

## Personal Vision

A wider range of prints in this exhibition reveals imagery which is not drawn from the social and physical world, but which is produced from more disparate or abstract sources. This imagery creates its own world, sometimes simply in terms of a two-dimensional abstract image formed through an interest in the sensuousness of formal properties such as colour (Graham Kuo), line (Grahame King), decorative symbols (John Coburn), forms in space (Alun Leach-Jones), or marks and surfaces (Allan Mitelman, John Neeson, Stephen Spurrier, to some degree Tim Storrier and Robert Grieve, and in a special sense as already indicated, Fred Williams). In the more particular cases of private fantasy (Petr Herel), or personal vision (Jock Clutterbuck, Jan Senbergs, Greg Moncrieff, Colin Lanceley, Jim Taylor), a world constructed from odd juxtapositions has the presence of a new reality with its own coherence and logic.

In the prints by **Greg Moncrieff** and **Jim Taylor** the intrusions of aspects of everyday reality produce images that are often already emotionally loaded — Taylor's frightened rabbits and Moncrieff's holiday palm trees, or bandages with their associations of pain — which seem to function as leftovers of an ordinary world. They carry their emotional loadings into a world that does not necessarily endorse them and certainly does not always fully explain them.

The metaphor of the rabbits in *Colonial Impression* is fairly explicit but the statement is not merely doctrinaire. *Boolara Campsite* is more elusive. A slight sense of tension derives from the rabbit with the hunted look edging in from the left corner into an anonymous environment. When the dark velvety blue sweep of plain colour finds its edge, this analogy to a horizon line suggests a sky in the light blue upper section, while the fumes which emerge mysteriously from the crumpled paper bag drift up across it to suggest another illusion of natural space in an oddly unnatural environment. The crumpled cloth and two paper bags, objects isolated like the rabbit, beg the question of their content or purpose. The nature of their depiction and the quality of the drawing seems to intensify an expectation that they do have a purpose and provides them with a personality. The paper bag with the torn edges (a little like ears), seems to counter the rabbit on the right. And so we have an image in which an environment is landscaped by objects, remnants of man's leisure, and the photographic fragments of the living rabbit seem as alien in it as they.

Greg Moncrieff juxtaposes images and motifs (drawn or photographic), but first leeches them of some of their realism by dropping out a midtone or colour, as in the packet of dwarf bean seeds in *Tahiti — Not What It Used To Be*. Here the sense of artifice is consciously apparent. The source of the scenery photo is obviously a magazine or tourist brochure — as the fold down the middle allows us to see. The grainy surface of the blow-up and the bleak monochrome deprive Tahiti of its customary allure and the other

three images placed across the photo seem oddly incongruous to this environment. If some of the juxtapositions prompt associations, such as the potential "stringless tender crop" next to the enduring palm tree, these associations are strangely unfruitful and resist pushing to any explicit formulations. The tightly drawn diagonal grid, and the lusher softness of blue primary coloured "rainbow" stripes within the keyhole shape, recur throughout Moncrieff's recent work, almost as personal motifs, autographed reminders of two different styles of image-making; so does the device of retaining the image of the masking tape. All these are reminders of artifice. The steps taken to create this new composite image remain undisguised, and Tahiti, the mecca of so many image-makers, is not what it used to be.

The quality of the line is the most important means by which **Petr Herel** and **Murray Walker** create their private world. Walker's world is obviously derived from a social reality: random observations from the streets which meander in new confrontations on his page. They have the quality of private diary jottings. In *Vignettes : Entertainers At Rest* the motif of the kiss has an animal quality, so different from Bea Maddock's cooler images. The mouths devour each other and there is a vulgar vitality which slips into decadence. The loose, nervous, seemingly automatic line forms figures which spill over the page. As the line strengthens, in some areas slight recession is suggested for the lighter figures but generally there is no sense of space. Thus there is no sense of a world in which these encounters and juxtapositions might take place, except that of Walker's vision. Yet the sharp observation of expression and posture cause us to recognise the world from which they emerge in flashes of caricature. In this sense Walker's erotic images are clearly tied to a social reality in a way that Petr Herel's are not.

## Signs and Ideas

**Ruth Faerber** is interested in the relationship of marks on surfaces, but metaphysical concerns also generate her images. She states that:

> The stimulating challenge of printmaking lies in making discoveries within a technical framework. This is what excites me. Lithography as a medium appeals to me because of its direct spontaneous quality — the mark becomes the print. My images develop more often than not out of the discoveries I make during the process only conditioned and refined by a search for form and space relationships. However, underlying these formal considerations, is my constant thought of life as a continuum and an awareness of the catatonic journey of every man. Complexities of evolution, subtleties of communication, delicious pangs of solitude — perhaps these are what my work is about.[15]

Subtleties of communication isolated in a pervading solitude are conveyed in both of Faerber's prints included here, but perhaps more explicitly in *Oriental Vibrations,* where physical fragments of a real world are isolated in a space created by the artist. In a warm image silver paper is overprinted in gold with tiny dots of rich mauves and pinks, blues and reds that radiate outwards through the confines of squares. There is an illusion of warm air expanding and vibrating around the dots and, as the colours seem to rise, the rectangle becomes a floating carpet. In this context the real fragments of the physical world have a particular tangibility, unlike the use of collage in Tim Storrier's *The Flag, Camp At Relay,* where imagined shapes seem to grow out of real counterparts and the ambiguity between printed and real surfaces and forms is continually created in their constant reiteration of each other. In *Oriental Vibrations* the drift of the orange feather suggests a journey across vast space. The photographic image of the physical world — the small yet direct and immediate image of the smiling face of a young Chinese woman seems to be simultaneously a fragment of the sources generating these vibrations, and yet also seems caught within them herself.

The use of inscriptions in the work of **Ray Beattie** and **Arthur Wicks** suggests an interest in conceptual ideas. Both are concerned with systems of understanding. The dry precise spidery quality of the line in the monochrome etching, with its pale screenprinted title of *The Source For A Great Idea,* sets up a graph-like background for the dark folds of the brain depicted like a mysterious convoluted bag. But this "Illustrated Understanding Of Whole Systems" as the work is subtitled, is neatly parodied by the words that issue from the source's mouth — "Look out Ray!"

In *Skeletal Hands* the static formality of the style — an invitation to scientific logic and neutrality — is countered, not by parody, but by a haunting contrast. The image thus produced is a silent protest that avoids sentimentality. The remnants of man, the forceful forearms of a human skeleton, grasp downwards into the harder ledge-like shapes whilst the fragile tapered joints of the whale with their delicate sweeping curves hang across the net. Fine precision of drawing and the numbering of finger joints act as code references, introducing a distancing perspective for the viewer which is belied by the force of the specific visual comparison and second inscription. Ray Beattie has stated, "I do not want to claim too much from universal logics, hence the denial of specific light sources and some perspectives."[16] This comment relates most explicitly to techniques used in his less diagrammatic works, but it is also clearly appropriate in different ways to the theme of these prints.

Arthur Wicks' images have the quality of a private exercise book concerned with systems for understanding the world. On one level the viewer responds to the works texturally; the ground of green yellow and brown dot marks have a totally different feeling to the dry formality of Beattie. There is an odd sense of contrast between the textural spontaneity of the hand prints left behind, tacky and awkward, as the photographed hand moves up the page, and the precision of technical instruments such as the compass. Attempts to grasp nature in both prints are recorded directly in action by the inclusion of images of real hands and feet, and by the immediacy of little memos to the experimenter. The image centres more around attempts to grasp a system, rather than the systems themselves, which remain elusive.

Ray Beattie and Arthur Wicks are the only two printmakers whose approach to image-making in this exhibition is explicitly and self-referentially intellectual. In their concern with systems of understanding they confront the viewer with the issue of whether "the only real things in this world are ideas". To return to the framework of Aurier's statement it is clear that in these prints objects do "have importance only as signs of ideas" — in marked contrast to the first group of prints discussed where a fascination with the object centres and locks its significance in the idiosyncratic recreation of its form.

Alison French, Melbourne 1979.

1 Radford, Ron — *Outlines of Australian Printmaking*
Ballarat Fine Art Gallery, Ballarat, Victoria, 1976.

2 Earle Backen exhibiting in this exhibition worked at Hayters Atelier 17 in Paris and contributed much stimulus to experimental approaches to techniques in the intaglio process, both as an artist and teacher at East Sydney Technical College. Janet Dawson, went abroad on a National Gallery School Scholarship and worked at the Atelier Patris in Paris where she printed lithographs of School of Paris painters such as Sugai and Corneille, returning to Melbourne where she established an important print workshop.

3 Hanrahan, Barbara — "A Self Portrait", *Imprint*, No. 3, 1978,
Print Council of Australia, Melbourne, Victoria.

4 Thomas, Daniel — *Australian Print Survey*
Art Gallery of New South Wales, Sydney, New South Wales, 1963.

5 Seidel, Brian — *Printmaking*, The Arts In Australia Series,
Longmans Green and Co. Ltd., Croydon, Victoria, 1965.

Mollison, James — "Printmaking In Australia", *Art and Australia*, Vol. 1, No. 4, February 1964.

Plant, Margaret — "Melbourne Printmakers", *Art Bulletin of Victoria*, 1973/74.

Kempf, Franz — *Contemporary Australian Printmakers*
Lansdowne Press, Melbourne, Victoria, 1976.

6 Kolenberg, Hendrik — *Ten Western Australian Printmakers*, The Western Australian Art Gallery, Perth, Western Australia, 1978.

7 Lynn, Elwyn — *Australian Painting*, Current Affairs Bulletin, Vol. 37, No. 1, Department of Adult Education, University of Sydney, NSW, 22 December 1965.

8 — *Ibid.*, p. 9.

9 Melville, Robert — *The Architectural Review*, April 1963, quoted *Ibid*, p. 11.

10 Newton, Eric — *The Manchester Guardian*, June 5, 1961, quoted *Ibid*, p. 9.

11 Williams, Fred — Interviewed by Patrick McCaughey *The Age*, Melbourne, June 3, 1978.

12 Aurier, Albert — "Symbolism in Painting : Paul Gauguin", *Mercure de France* (Paris) 1891, 159-164, trans. Rookmaaker and Chipp. Chipp, Herschel : *Theories of Modern Art — A Source Book by Artists and Critics*, University of California Press, Berkely, 1971, p. 90.

13 Ewington, Julie — Political Postering In Australia, *Imprint*, No. 1, 1978, Print Council of Australia.

14 Hanrahan — *Op.Cit.*, p. 5.

15 Kempf — *Op.Cit.*, p. 52.

16 Gough, Craig — Ray Beattie, *Imprint*, No. 1, 1977, Print Council of Australia, p. 3.


**Front cover:** Etching press
Stylized Australian flag

**Inside front cover:**
cat. 21 "Movement Five" (detail)
by Roger Kemp

**Pages 2 & 3**
cat. 11 "China Passage" (detail)
by Ruth Faerber

**Page 4**
cat. 2 "Images" (detail)
by Ray Arnold

**Page 9**
cat. 4 "Cartuja II" (detail)
by Earle Backen

**Page 11**
cat. 6 "Skeletal Hands" (detail)
by Ray Beattie

**Back cover:**
cat. 51 "Visiting Spinebill" (detail)
by David Rose

cat. 69 "Wild Dog Creek 1" (detail)
by Fred Williams

Image size (height x width)

Abbreviations
B.A.T. — Bon à Tirer (first print pulled when artist is satisfied with finished plate)

ACT     Australian Capital Territory
NSW     New South Wales
Qld     Queensland
SA      South Australia
Vic     Victoria
PCA     Print Council of Australia

# Ray Arnold


Born Victoria 1950.
Studied Melbourne State College 1969-72;
Caulfield Institute of Technology, Melbourne 1976-78.
Participated group exhibitions Australia; PCA Student
Exchange (Europe 1977); 2nd Western Pacific Print
Biennale 1978.
Teaches secondary school, Melbourne, Vic.


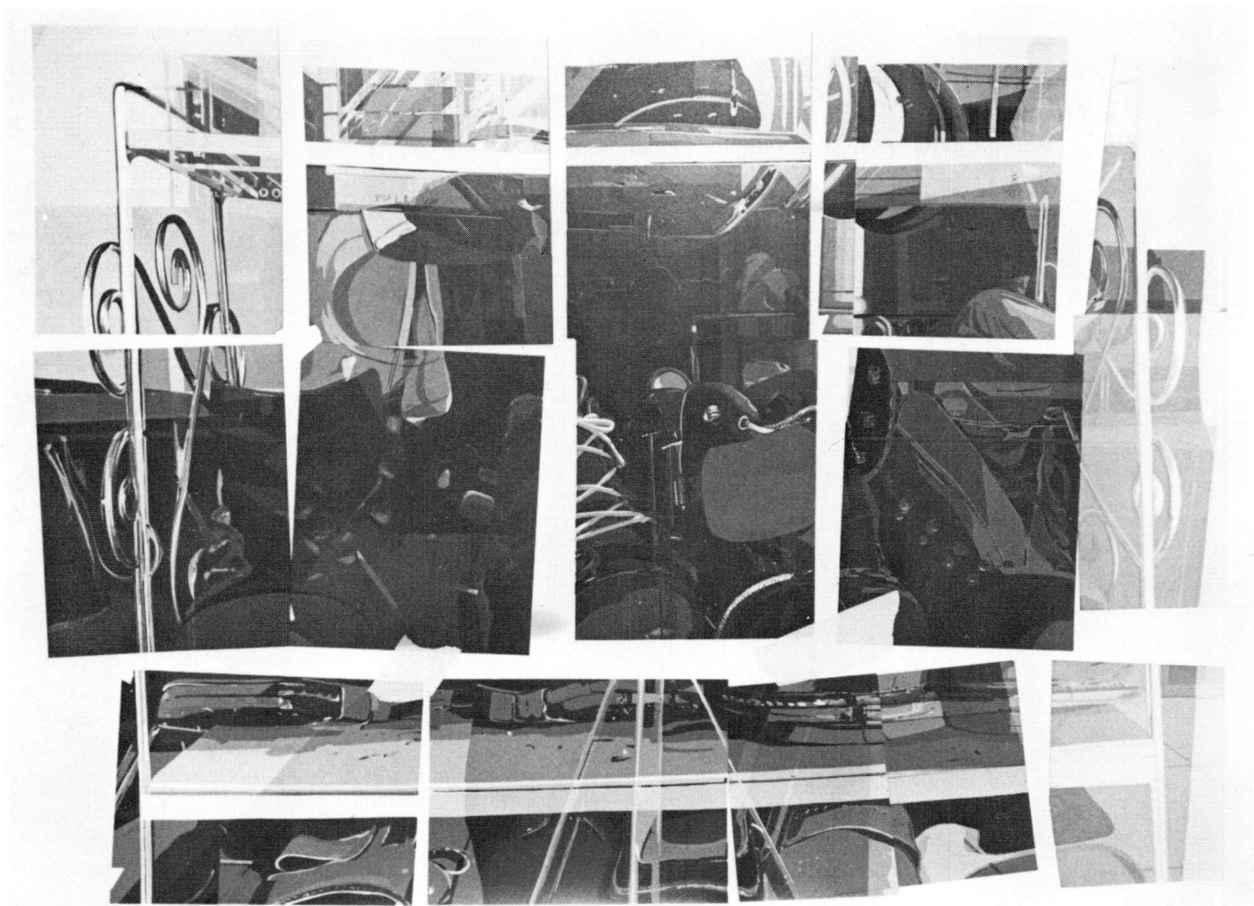

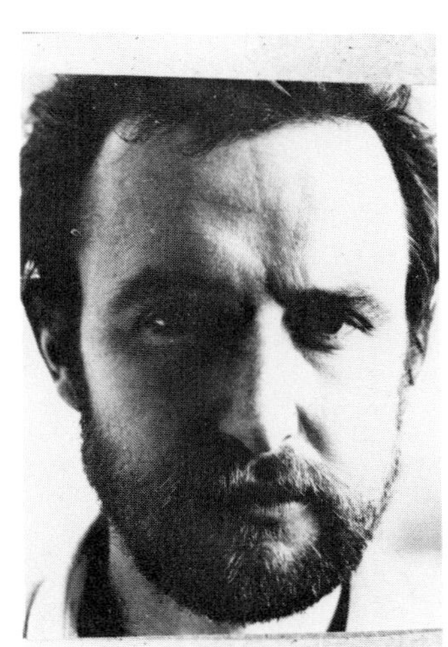

1 *Window For You*
   Screenprint       BFK Rives
   80 x 112 cm       Ed. 10

2 *Treason Of Images*
   Screenprint       BFK Rives
   79 x 115 cm       Ed. 14

# Earle Backen

Born New South Wales 1927.
Studied Central School of Arts & Crafts, Slade School,
London 1954; Atelier 17, Paris 1957.
Has held 14 one-man shows Australia.
Participated group exhibitions Australia; Philadelphia
Print Club (USA 1959); Cincinnati Biennale (USA 1960);
Smithsonian Institute Washington (USA 1966);
international print biennials (Japan 1960 '62; Poland
1962 '64 '70 '72).
Represented: Australian State and regional galleries;
Cincinnati Art Museum (USA).
PCA Patron Print edition commissioned 1975.
Teaches Alexander Mackie College of Advanced
Education, Sydney, NSW.

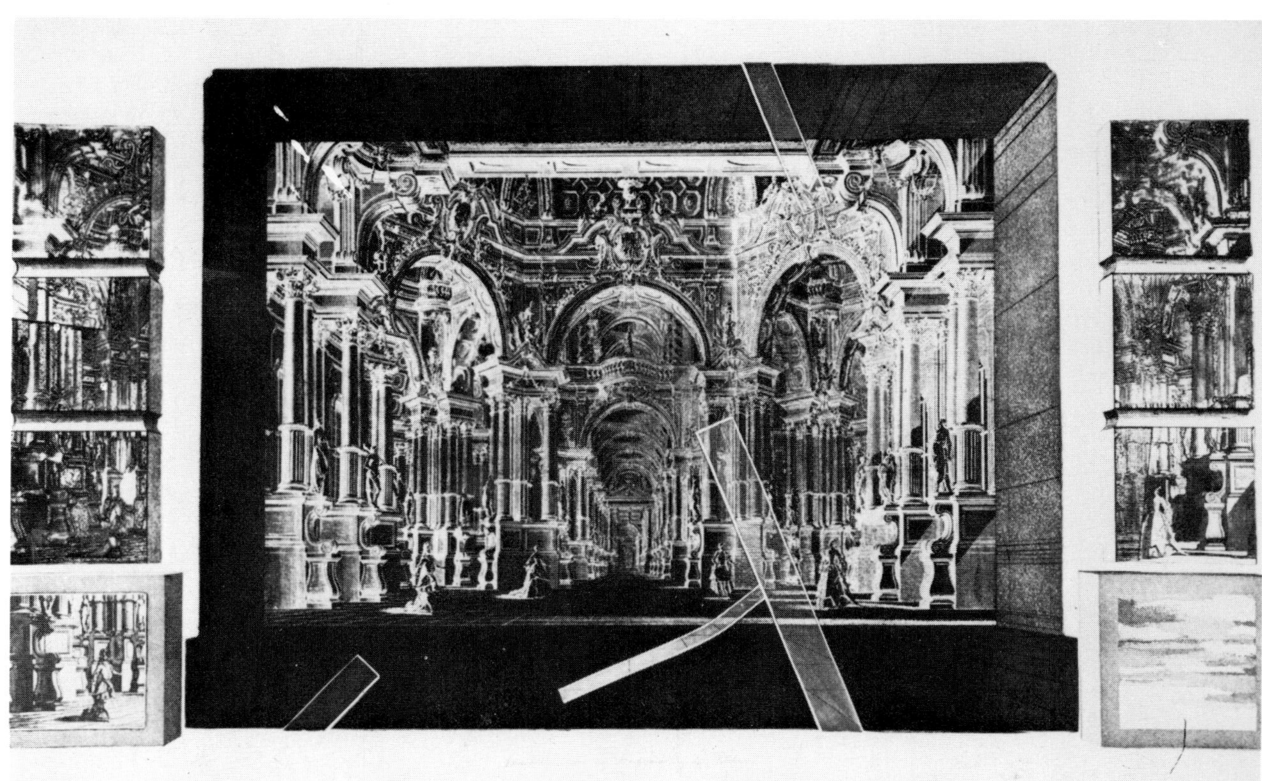

3

3 *Variation On An Engraving By Bibiena*
  Etching          BFK Rives
  47 x 86 cm    Ed. 25

4 *Cartuja II*
  Etching          BFK Rives
  61 x 45 cm    Ed. 25

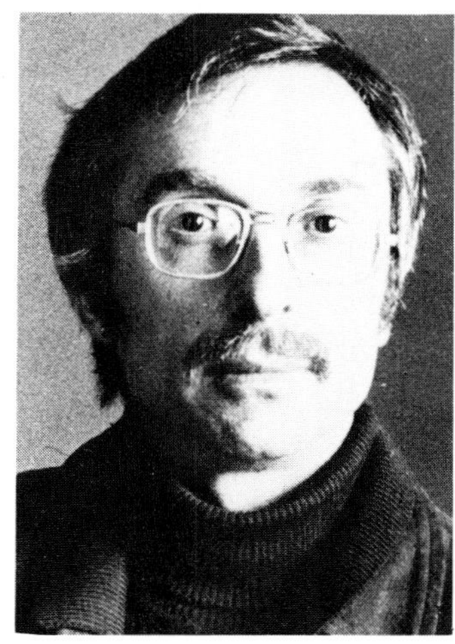

# Ray Beattie

Born Ireland 1949; arrived Australia 1967.
Largely self-taught, studied Fine Art (WA 1972-73);
The Victorian College of the Arts, 1978.
Has held 6 one-man shows, Australia.
Participated group exhibitions Australia; 1st Western
Pacific Print Biennale 1976.
Represented: Australian National Gallery (ACT); State
and regional galleries; educational institutions.
PCA Patron Print edition commissioned 1977.
Teaches Western Australian Institute of Technology,
Perth, WA.

5 *The Source Of A Great Idea (from An
Illustrated Understanding Of Whole Systems)*
Etching/screenprint   Arches Creme
22 x 22 cm        B.A.T.

6 *Skeletal Hands (from An Illustrated
Understanding Of Whole Systems)*
Etching        Arches Creme
20 x 20 cm     B.A.T.



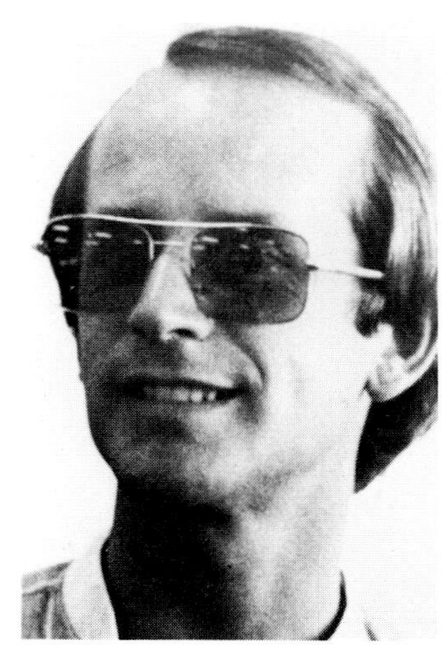

# Jock Clutterbuck

Born Victoria 1945.
Studied Royal Melbourne Institute of Technology 1965-66.
Has held one-man shows, Australia.
Participated group exhibitions Australia; Victoria and Albert Museum (London 1972); 4th International Print Biennale (Poland 1972); 111 International Print Biennale (Italy 1972); 9th Print Biennale (Japan 1974); 1st Western Pacific Print Biennale 1976.
Represented: Australian National Gallery (ACT); State and regional galleries; Museum of Modern Art (New York).
PCA Patron Print edition commissioned 1970.
Lectures The Victorian College of the Arts.

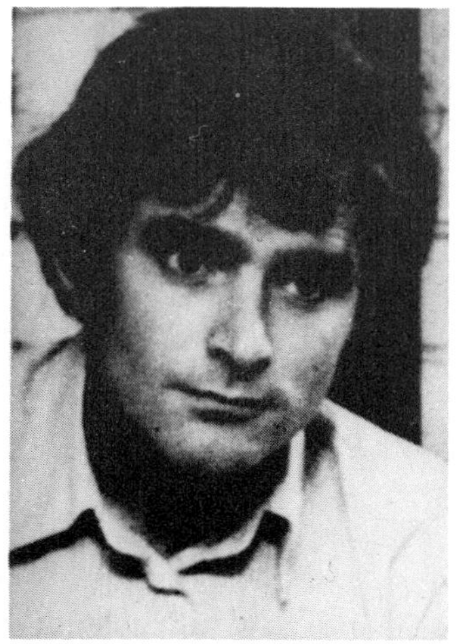

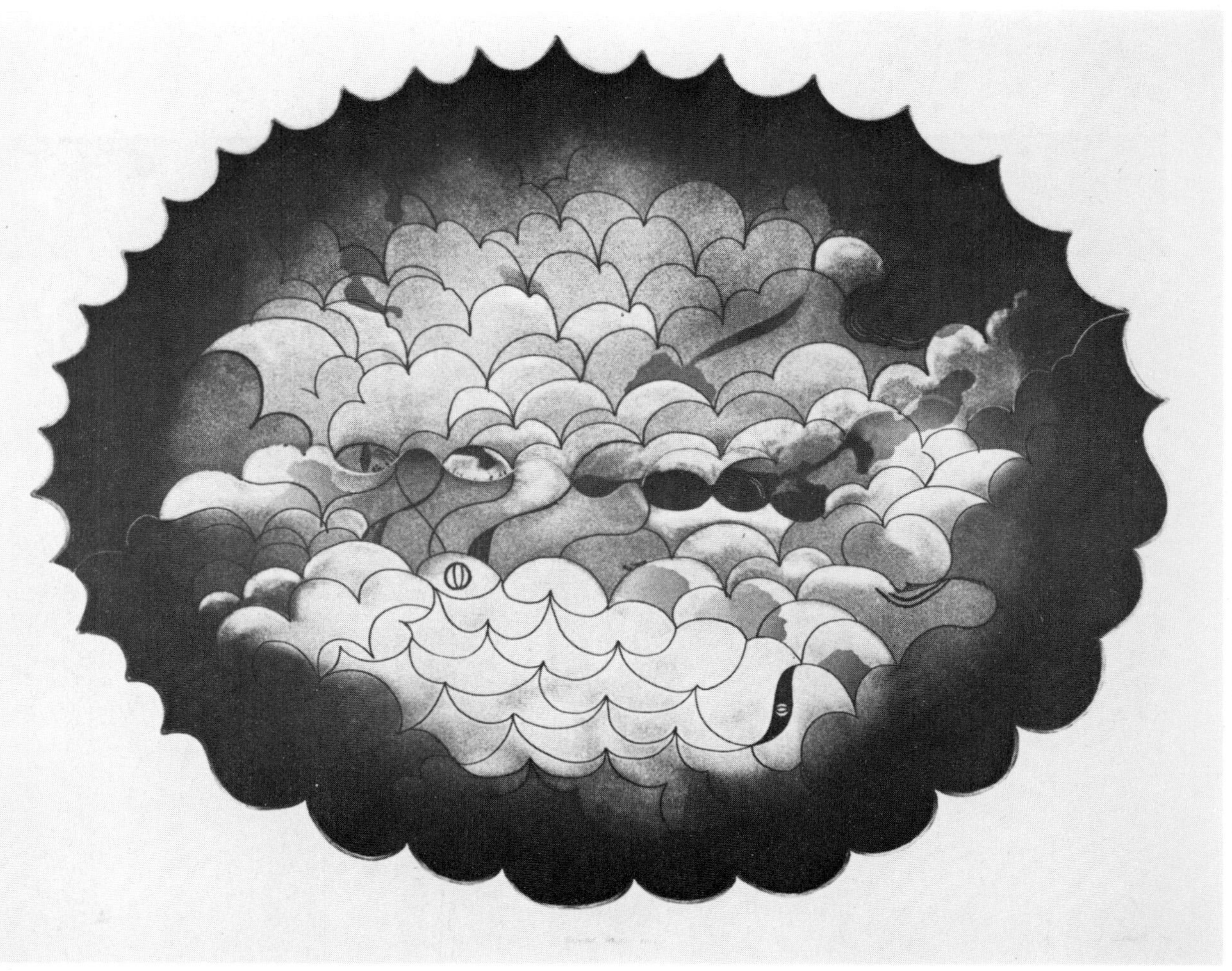



7 *Caves Of Wiswas No. 1*
  Etching          Torinoko
  65 x 86 cm    Ed. 20

8 *Crossfire*
  Etching          Torinoko
  87 x 60 cm    Ed. 20

# John Coburn

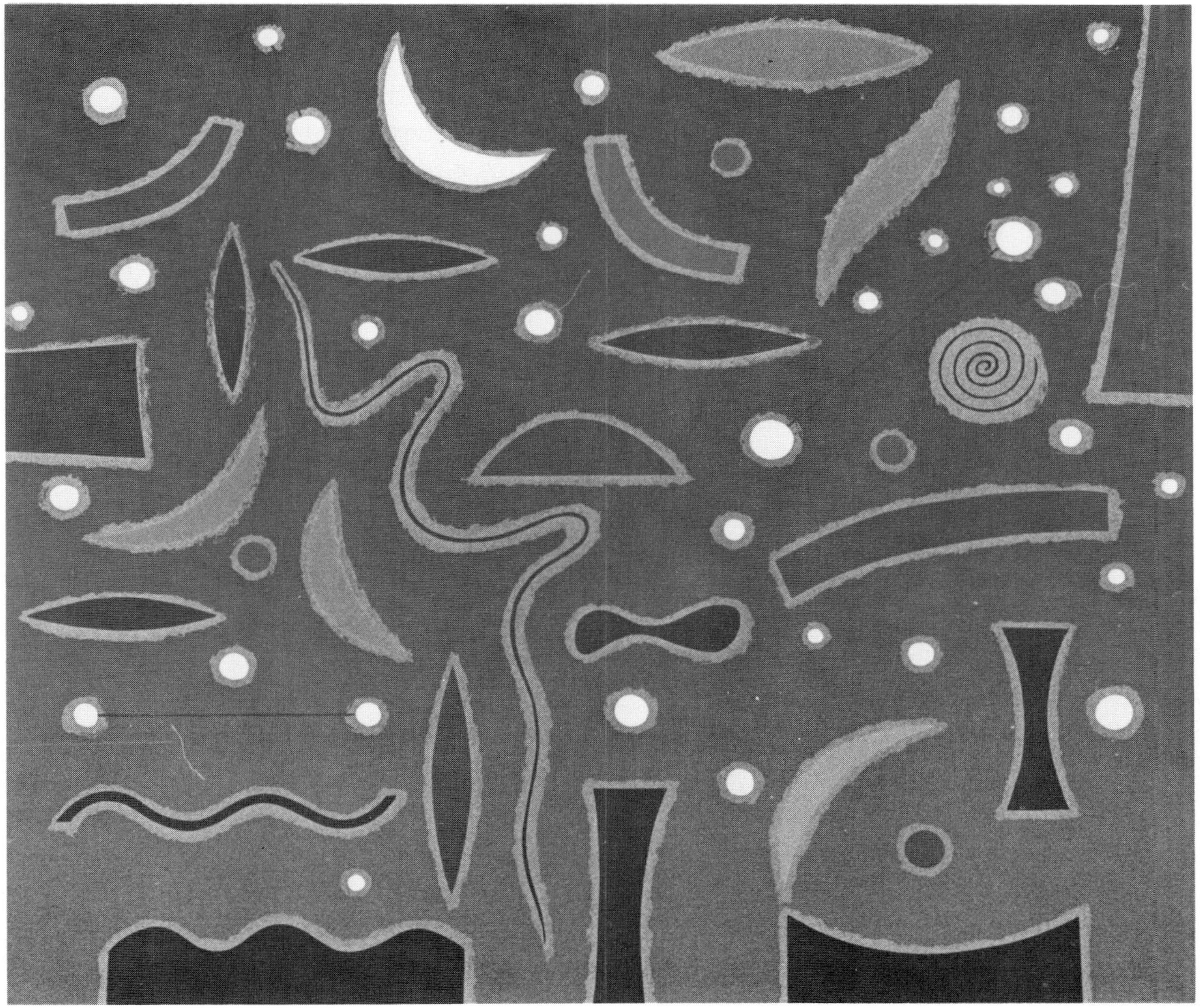

Born Queensland 1925.
Studied East Sydney Technical College 1947-50;
designed tapestries for Aubusson workshops (France
1969-72).
Has held 40 one-man shows Australia; France; USA.
Participated group exhibitions Australia; international
print biennials (Japan 1960; South America).
Represented: Australian National Gallery (ACT); State
and regional galleries; Vatican Museum (Italy);
Graphische Sammlung Albertina (Austria); John F.
Kennedy Centre (USA); University of Texas (USA).
Lives and works Sydney, NSW.

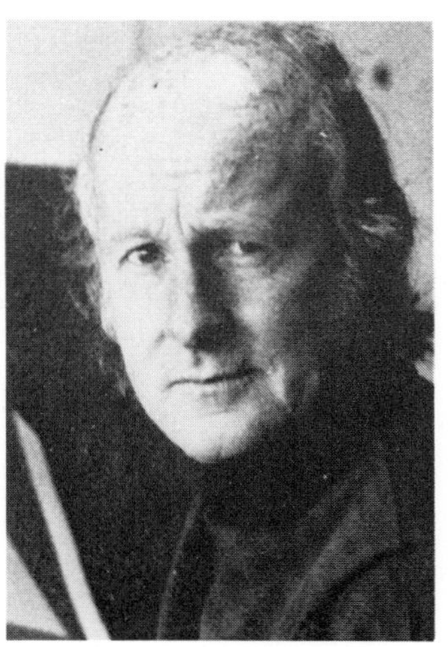

9  *Starry Night*
   Screenprint      Arches Aquarelle
   48 x 58 cm       Ed. 40

10  *Bright Day*
    Screenprint      Arches Aquarelle
    48 x 58 cm       Ed. 40

# Ruth Faerber



Born Sydney 1922.
Studied Commercial Art, Sydney 1938-40; Orban's
Studio, Sydney 1943-45; further studies with Orban and
East Sydney Technical College 1951-62; North Shore
Arts Centre (NSW) 1961-67; Pratt Centre (New York) 1968.
Has held 15 one-man shows Australia; New Zealand.
Participated group exhibitions Australia; International
Print Biennale, Bradford (UK 1969).
Represented: Australian State and regional galleries;
Bezalel Museum (Israel).
PCA Member Print edition commissioned 1974.
Lives and works Sydney, NSW.

11 *China Passage*
   Lithograph/collage      Aluminium laminate on
                           Filter paper
   41 x 52 cm              Ed. 10

12 *Oriental Vibrations*
   Lithograph/collage      Aluminium laminate on
                           Filter paper
   46 x 32 cm              Ed. 10

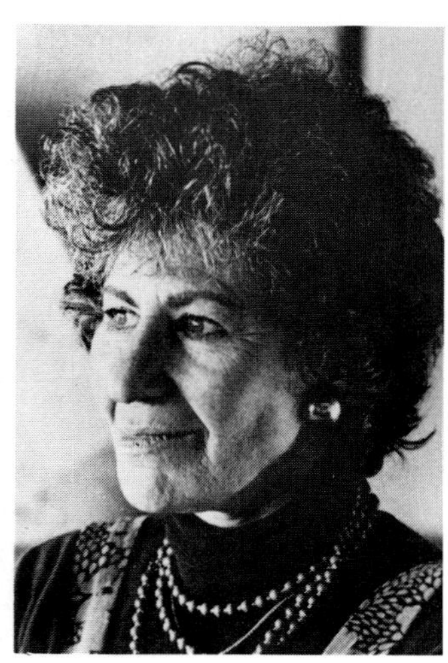

"

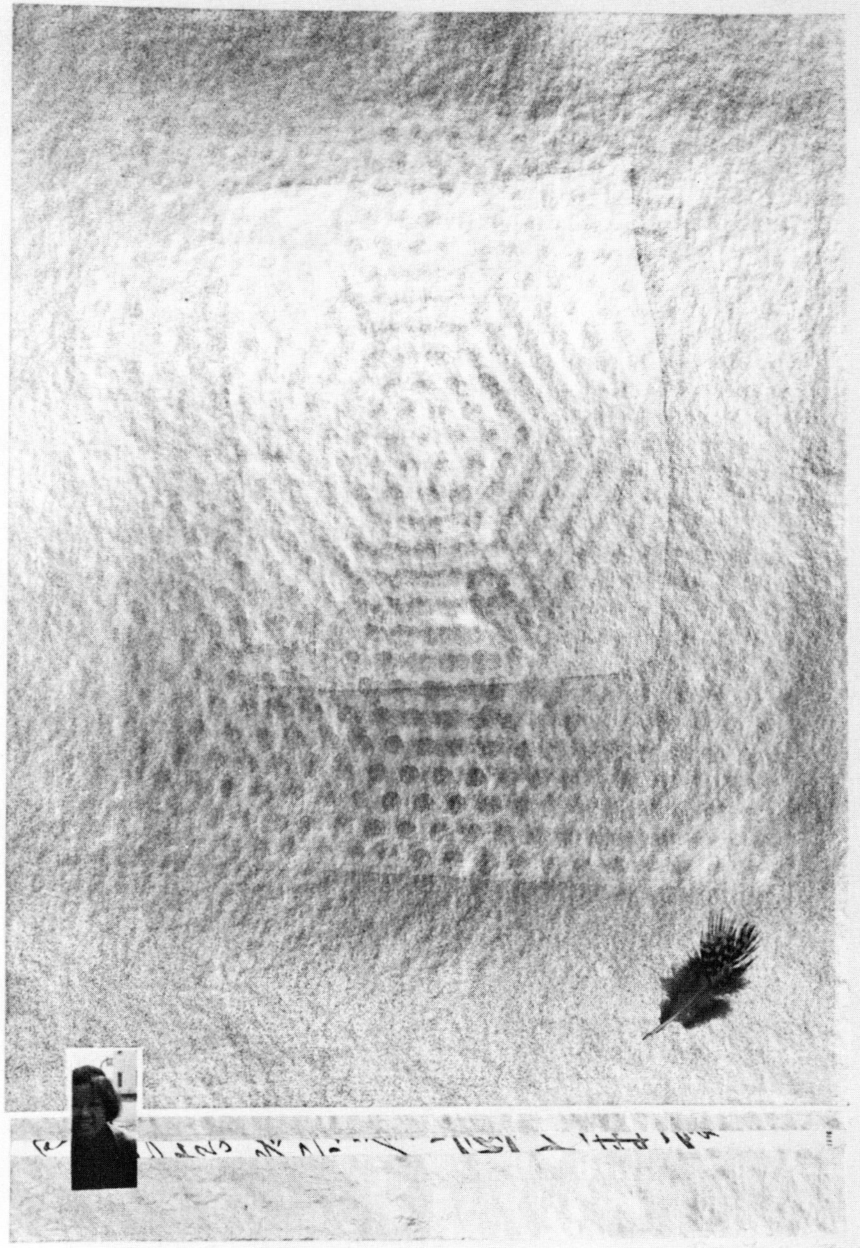

# Robert Grieve

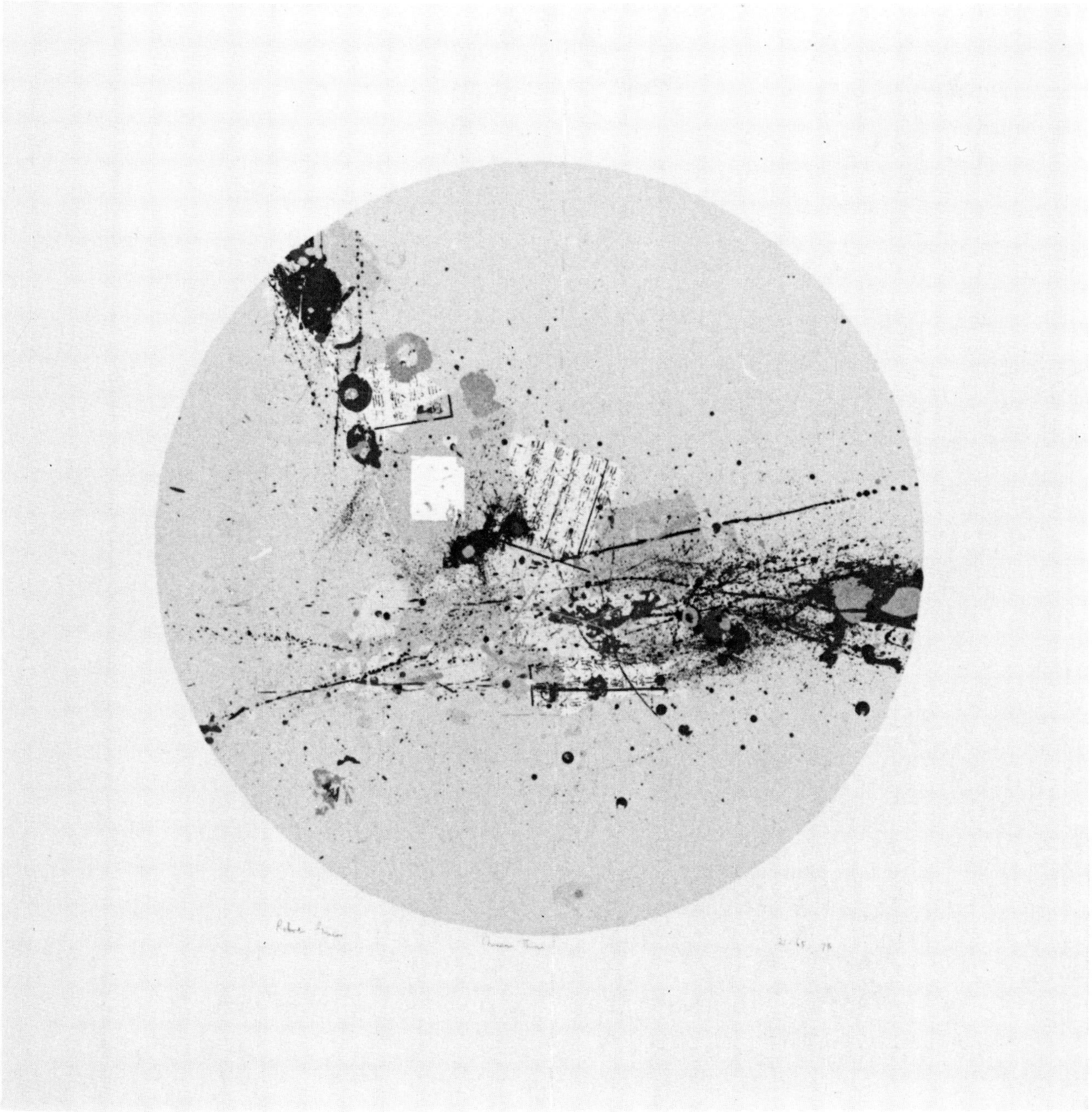

Born Melbourne 1924.
Studied Regent Polytechnic, London 1952-54.
Has held one-man shows Australia.
Participated group exhibitions Australia; International
Print Biennale (Japan 1962 '64); Australian Graphics
(Poland 1972-73); Six x Four (New Zealand 1975).
Represented: Australian State and regional galleries;
educational institutions; Japan Print Association; Vilnus
Art Gallery (USSR).
PCA Patron Print edition commissioned 1974.
Lives and works Melbourne, Vic.

13 *China Wall*
   Etching/collograph      Arches
   37 x 30 cm              Ed. 25

14 *Chinese Theme*
   Screenprint             Fabriano
   45 cm diameter          Ed. 65

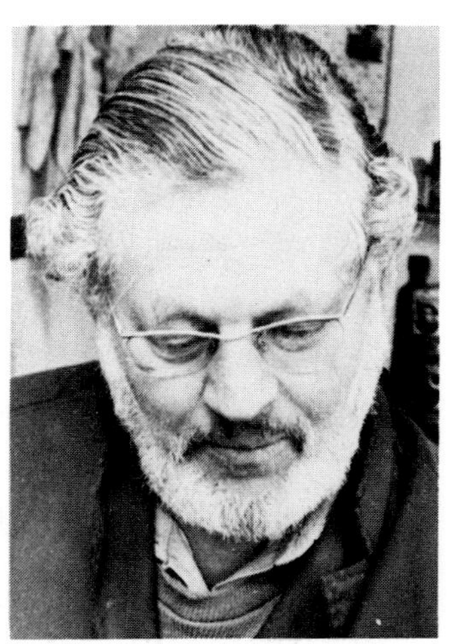

# Barbara Hanrahan

Born South Australia 1939.
Studied South Australian School of Art 1957-62;
Central School of Art, London 1963-66.
Has held 16 one-man shows Australia; London; Italy.
Participated group exhibitions Australia; Six x Four
(New Zealand 1975); 5th British International Print
Biennale (UK 1975); International Biella Prize for Prints
(Italy 1976); 1st Western Pacific Print Biennale 1976;
PCA Exhibition (Japan, Fiji 1977).
Represented: Australian National Gallery (ACT); State
and regional galleries; educational institutions; Greater
London Council; Japan Print Association.
PCA Member Print edition commissioned 1974.
Lives and works Adelaide, SA.

15  *Wedding Night*
   Screenprint    J. J. Head
   70 x 50 cm    Ed. 8

16  *Men And Women*
   Screenprint    Barcham Green
   80 x 57 cm    Ed. 24

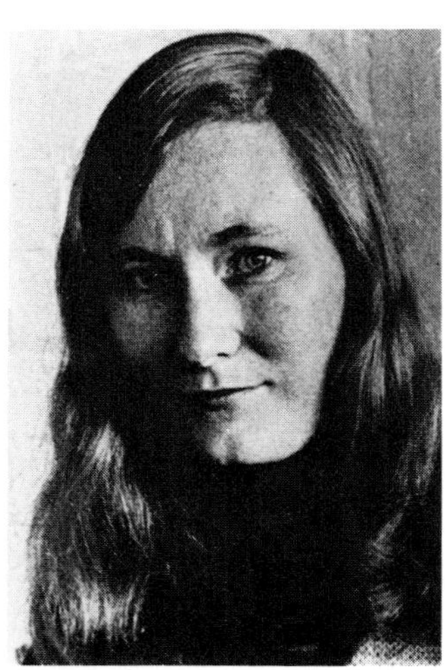

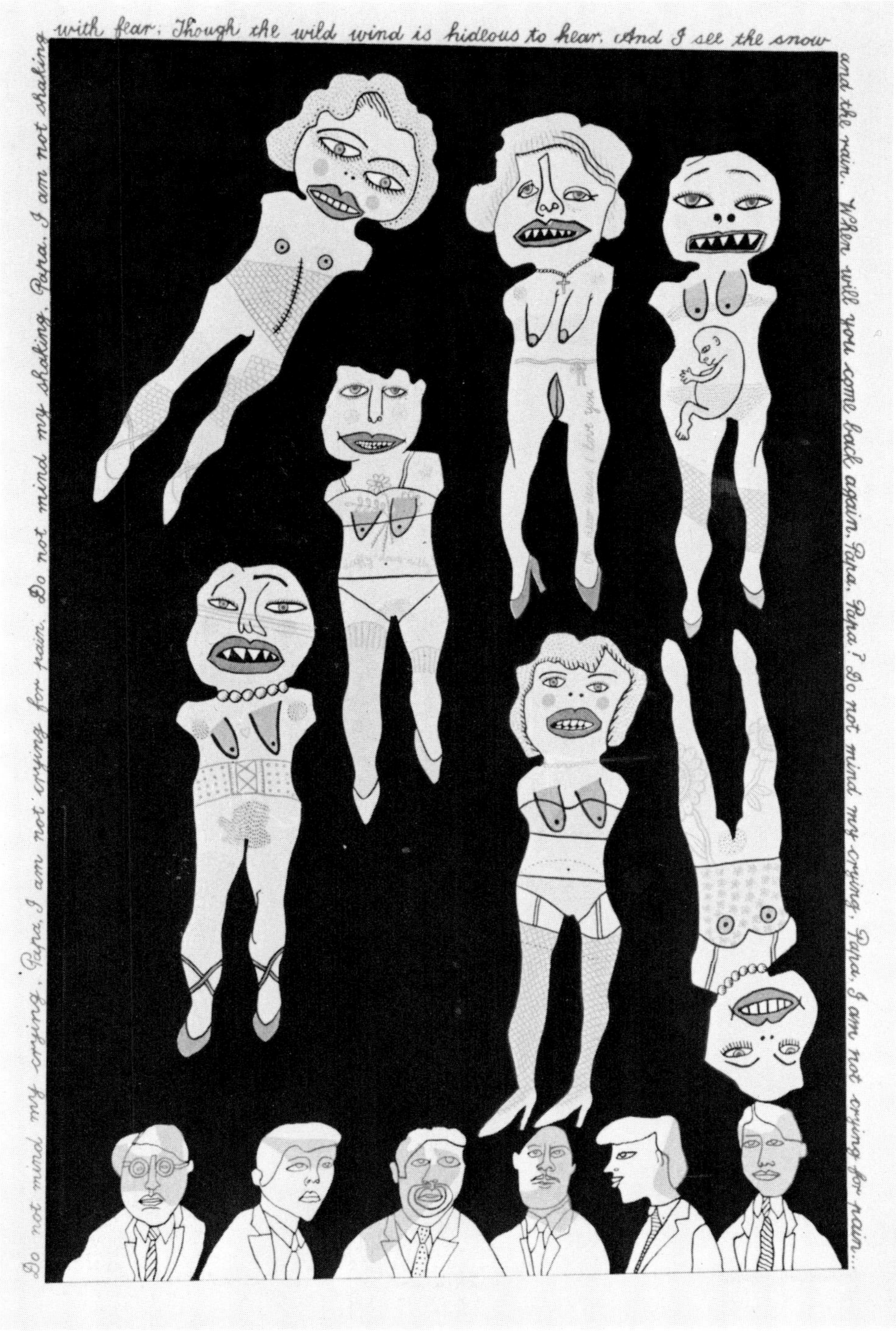

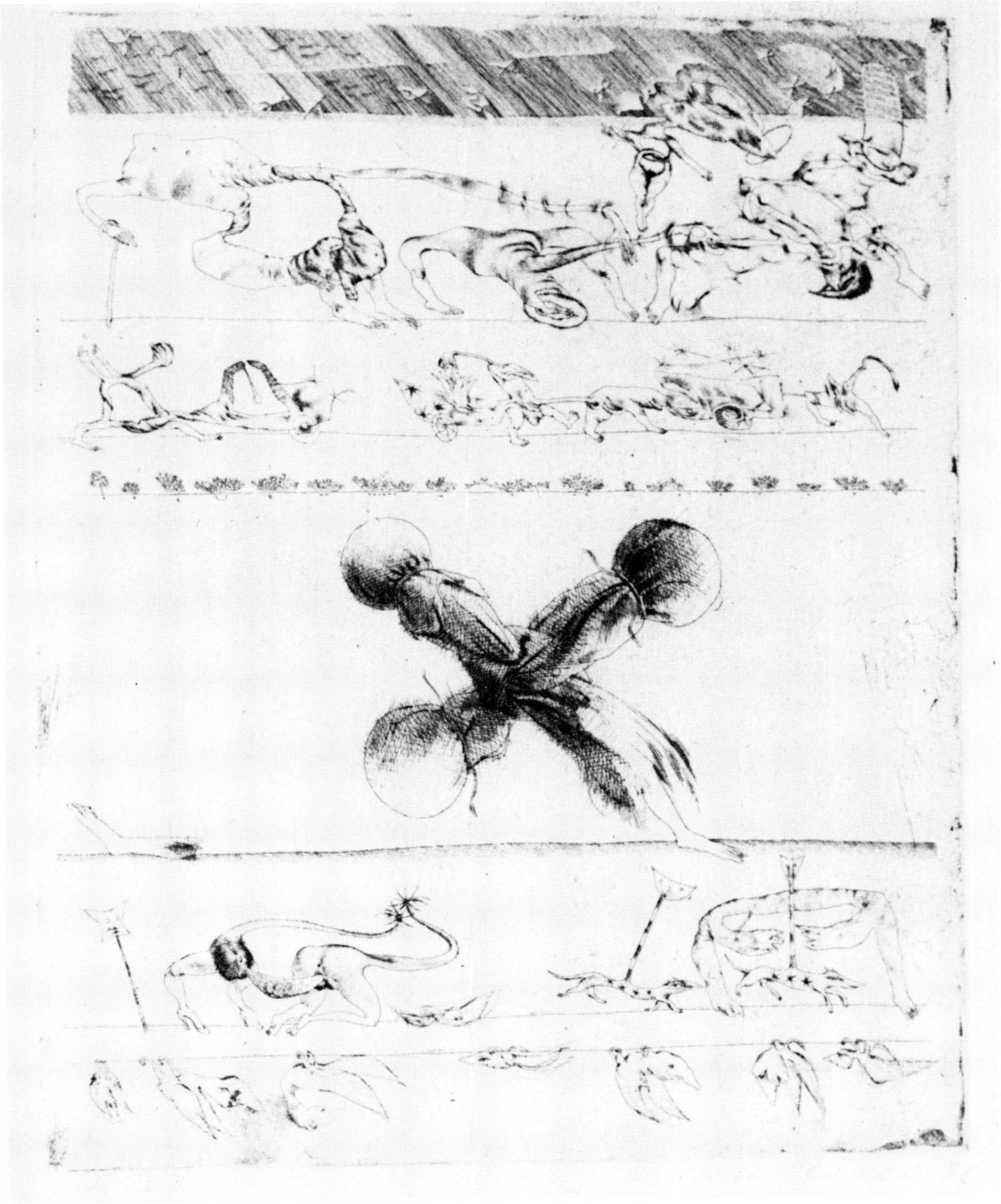

# Petr Herel

Born Czechoslovakia 1943.
Studied Prague College of Art 1957-61;
Prague University of Applied Arts 1964-69.
Has held 10 one-man shows Australia, Italy, France.
Participated group exhibitions Australia; Biennale of
Graphic Art (Yugoslavia 1973 '75); Premio
Internazionale for Engraving (Italy 1973); Bienal
Internacional of Graphic Art (Spain 1974); Art Festival
of Christchurch (New Zealand 1978).
Represented: Australian National Gallery (ACT); State
and regional galleries; Prague City Gallery
(Czechoslovakia); Mulhouse Bibliothèque (France).
PCA Patron Print edition commissioned 1976.
Lectures Canberra School of Art, ACT.

17 *Untitled*
   Etching          BFK Rives
   28 x 23 cm       Ed. 20

18 *Untitled*
   Etching          BFK Rives
   28 x 23 cm       Ed. 20

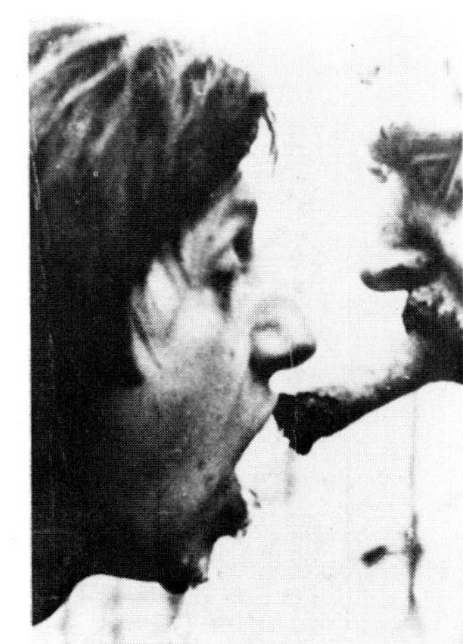

# William Kelly



Born New York 1943; arrived Australia 1968.
Studied Albright-Knox Art Gallery (USA); Philadelphia
College of Art (USA); Prahran Technical College,
Melbourne; National Gallery School of Art, Melbourne.
Has held 9 one-man shows Australia, USA, Italy.
Participated group exhibitions Australia; ''Seven Young
Artists'' (USA 1972); ''Watergate'' (Sweden, Denmark
1974).
Currently Dean, School of Art, The Victorian College of
the Arts.

19  *Person On Studio Floor (Male)*
    Lithograph     Arches
    68 x 50 cm     Ed. 20

20  *Person On Studio Floor (Female)*
    Lithograph     BFK Rives
    71 x 50 cm     Ed.     15

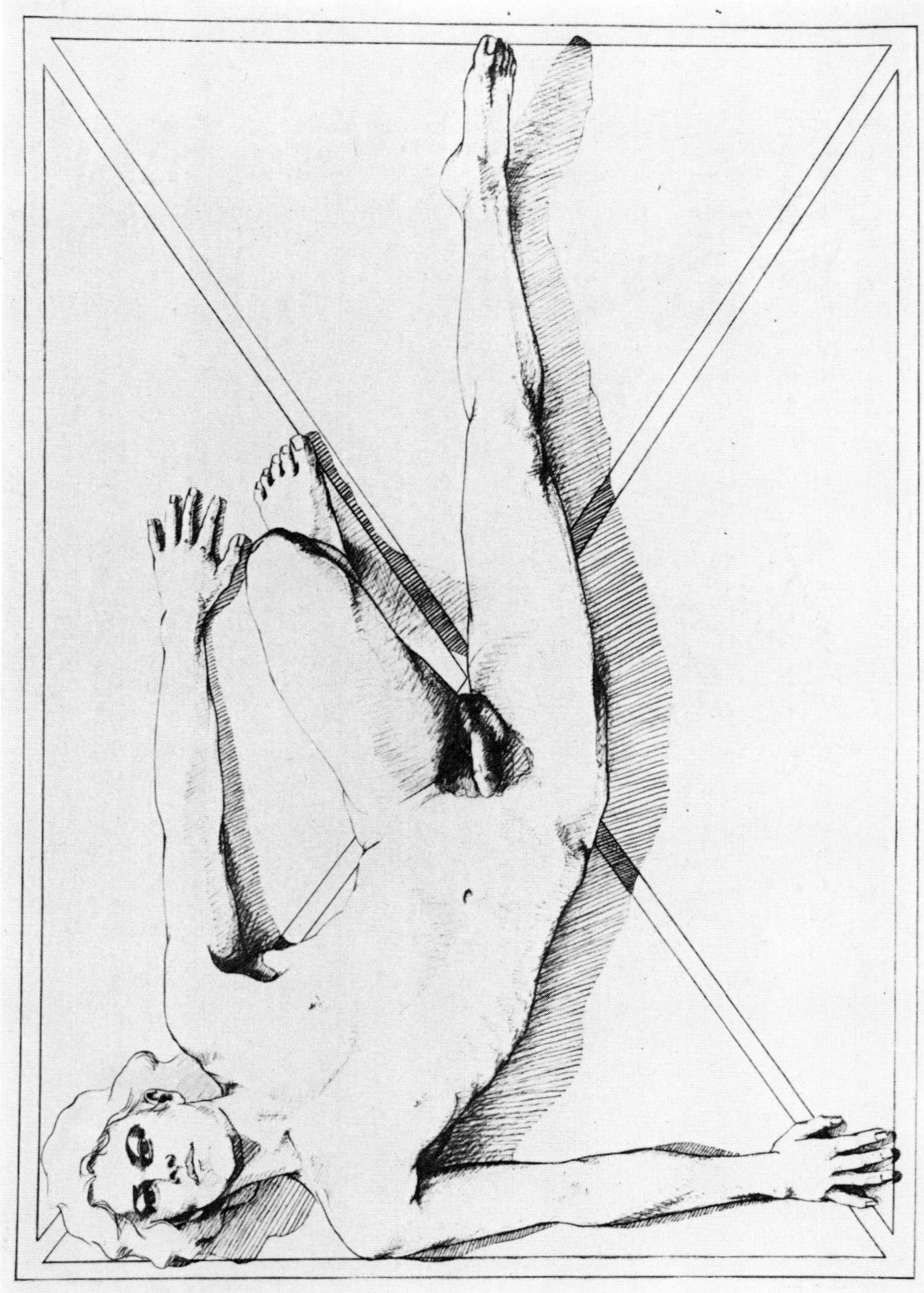

# Roger Kemp

Born Victoria 1908.
Studied National Gallery School, Melbourne;
Royal Melbourne Institute of Technology.
Has held one-man shows Australia, including
simultaneous retrospective five-gallery exhibition
(Melbourne 1978).
Participated group exhibitions Australia; Australian
Graphics (South America 1974); 1st Western Pacific
Print Biennale 1976; Japan Print Association (Japan
1977); PCA Exhibition (Japan, Fiji 1977).
Represented: Australian State and regional galleries.
PCA Patron Print edition commissioned 1976.
Lives and works Melbourne, Vic.

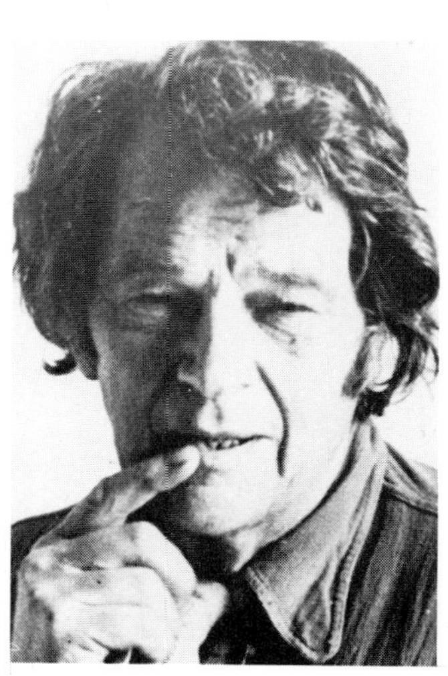

21 *Movement Five*
   Etching        Arches
   50 x 63 cm     A/P

22 *Horizontal Twelve*
   Etching        Arches
   50 x 89 cm     A/P

# Grahame King

Born Melbourne 1915.
Studied National Gallery School, Melbourne; post-graduate studies UK, Europe 1938-42;
Study tours UK, Japan.
Has held one-man shows Australia.
Participated group exhibitions Australia; 1st British International Print Biennale (UK 1969); PCA Exhibitions (SE-Asia, Poland, USA); 1st Western Pacific Print Biennale 1976.
Represented: Australian National Gallery (ACT); State and regional galleries; Victoria & Albert Museum (London).
PCA Patron Print edition commissioned 1971.
Foundation member and first honorary secretary, Print Council of Australia.
Lectures Royal Melbourne Institute of Technology, Vic.

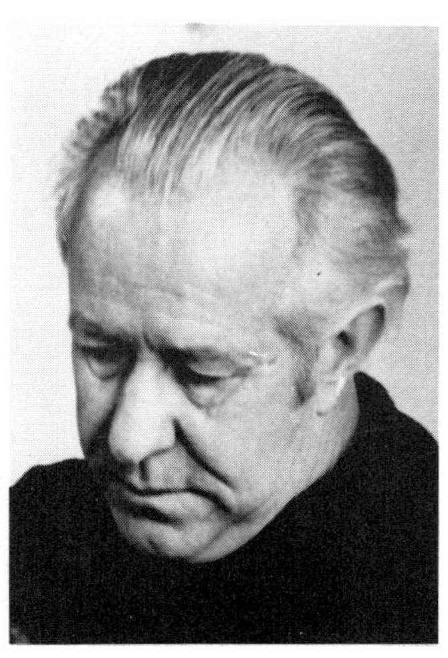

24

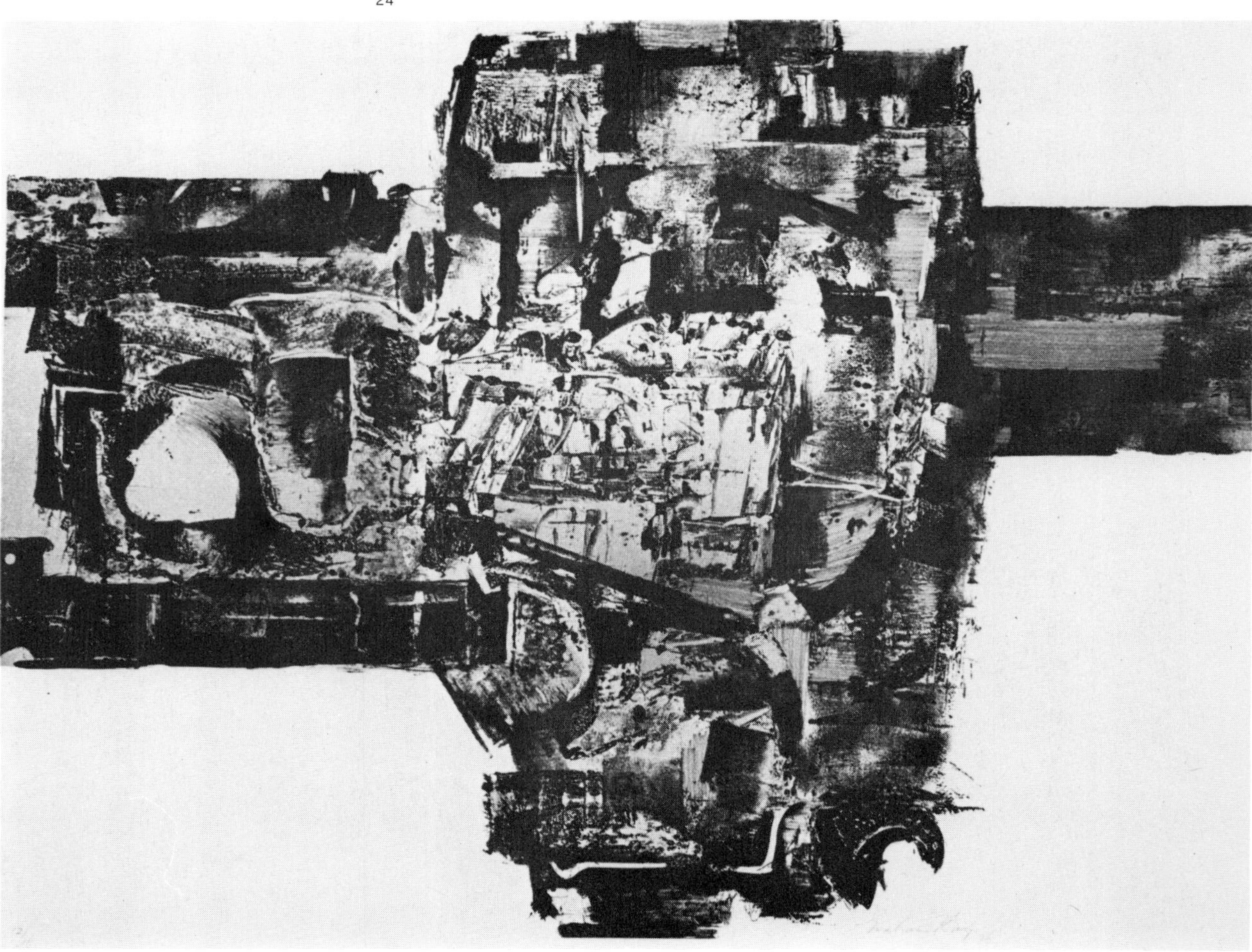

23 *East Wind*
   Lithograph    Arches Satine
   74 x 54 cm    Ed. 12

24 *Untitled*
   Lithograph    Arches Satine
   54 x 76 cm    Ed. 16

# Graham Kuo

Born China 1949.
Studied National Art School, Sydney 1968-70.
Has held 6 one-man shows Australia.
Participated group exhibitions Australia; Tokyo Print
Exhibition (Japan 1976); 1st Western Pacific Print
Biennale 1976; 7th International Print Biennale
(Poland 1978).
Represented: Australian State and regional galleries;
educational institutions.
PCA Member Print edition commissioned 1976.
Lives and works Sydney, NSW.

26

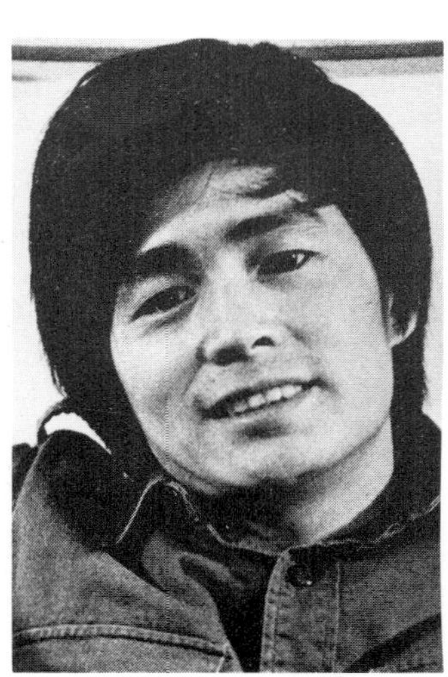

25 *Lingi Pink*
   Screenprint      Arches Velin
   75 x 105 cm      Ed. 17

26 *Brown Kario*
   Screenprint      Arches Velin
   75 x 105 cm      Ed. 17

# Geoff La Gerche

Born Victoria 1940.
Studied Caulfield Institute of Technology, Melbourne; Royal College of Art, London.
Has held 8 one-man shows Australia.
Participated group exhibitions Australia; Studio Prints (London 1969); Six x Four (New Zealand 1975); 1st Western Pacific Print Biennale 1976; Contemporary Australian Printmakers (Japan, Fiji 1977).
Represented: Australian State and regional galleries; educational institutions; Royal Commonwealth Society (London).
PCA Patron Print edition commissioned 1975.
Lectures Caulfield Institute of Technology, Vic.

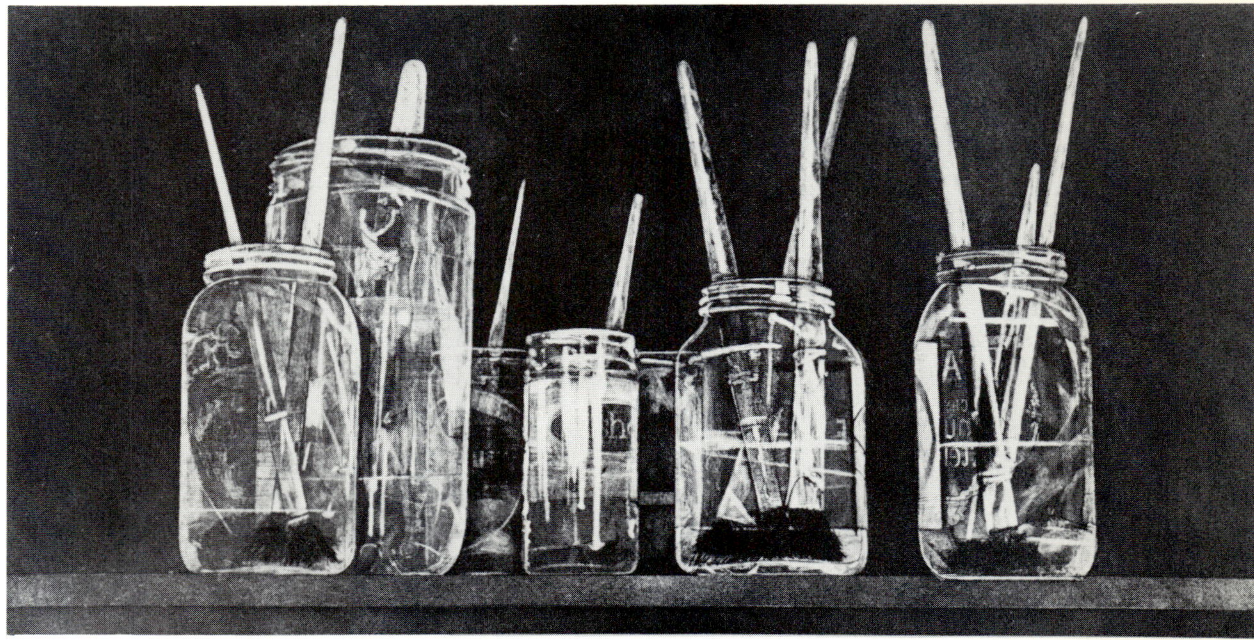

28

27  *Nine Brushes*
    Etching        Arches Creme
    41 x 100 cm    Ed. 15

28  *Jars And Brushes*
    Etching        Arches Creme
    50 x 100 cm    Ed. 15

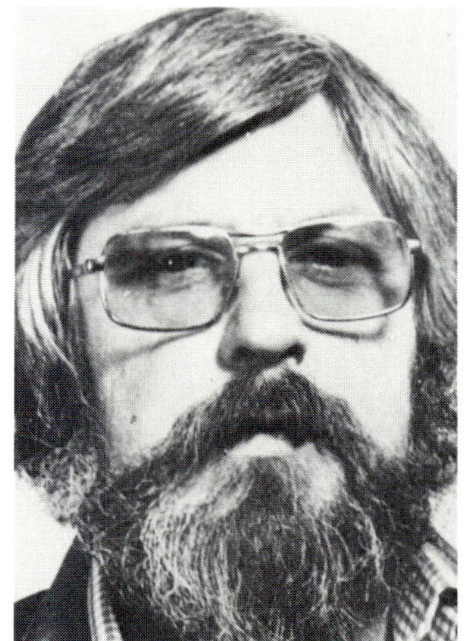

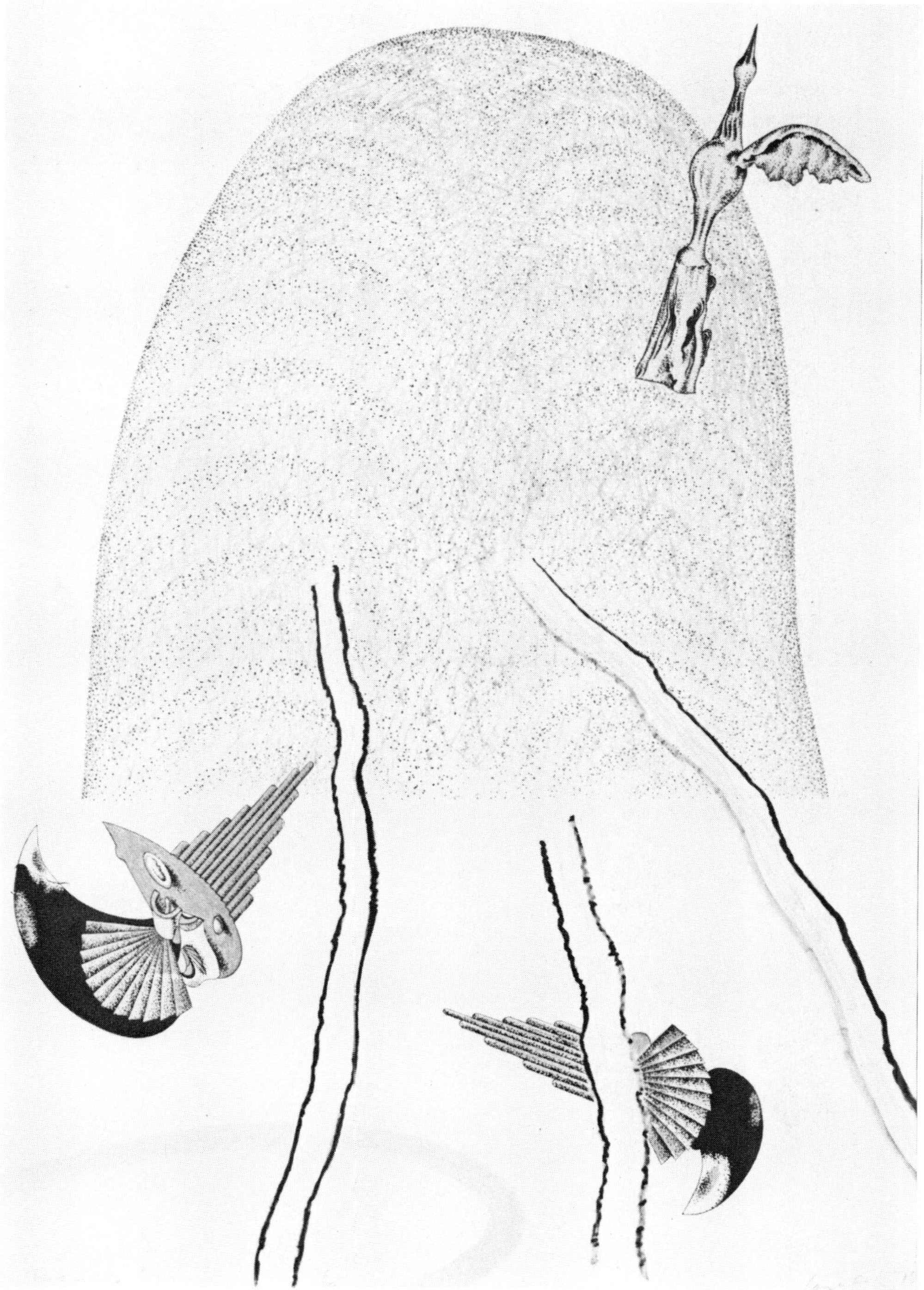

# Colin Lanceley

Born New Zealand 1938; arrived Australia 1940.
Studied East Sydney Technical College 1956-60.
Has held one-man shows Australia, UK, USA, Europe.
Participated group exhibitions Australia, UK, USA,
Poland, Japan, Canada.
Represented: Australian National Gallery (ACT); State
and regional galleries; Museum of Modern Art (New
York); Tate Gallery (London); Victoria & Albert Museum
(London); Centre National d'Art Contemporain (Paris);
Stedelijk Museum (Amsterdam); Bezalel National Art
Museum (Israel); National Museums of Cracow,
Warsaw, Poznan, and Musie Siliscenne (Poland);
National Museum (Germany).
Lives and works London, UK.

29  *The Empire Builder*
    Lithograph      Arches
    72 x 95 cm      Ed. 75

30  *Two In The Bush*
    Lithograph      Arches
    95 x 68 cm      Ed. 50

Courtesy Realities Gallery Vic

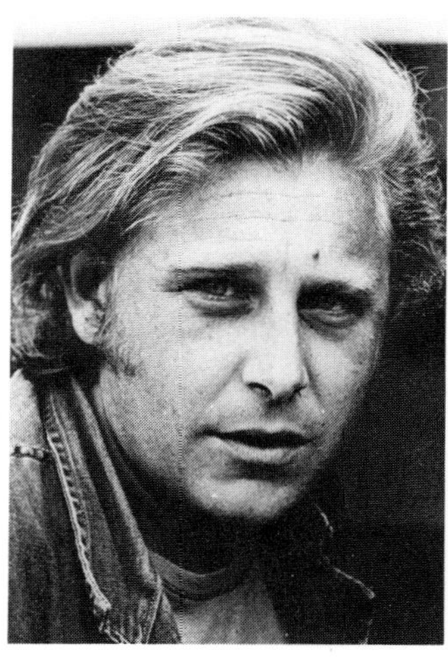

# Bruce Latimer

Born Sydney 1951.
Studied National Art School, Sydney 1970-73.
Has held 3 one-man shows Australia.
Participated group exhibitions Australia; PCA Exhibition (Japan, Fiji 1977); British International Print Biennale (Bradford, UK 1979).
Represented: Australian State and regional galleries; Noumea Art Gallery.
Lives and works Sydney, NSW.

31 *Black Out Print*
   Screenprint/collage     Fabriano
   77 x 56 cm              Ed. 50

32 *Guarded Thoughts/Different Dogs*
   Screenprint/collage     Fabriano
   56 x 77 cm             Ed. 47

   Courtesy Watters Gallery, NSW.

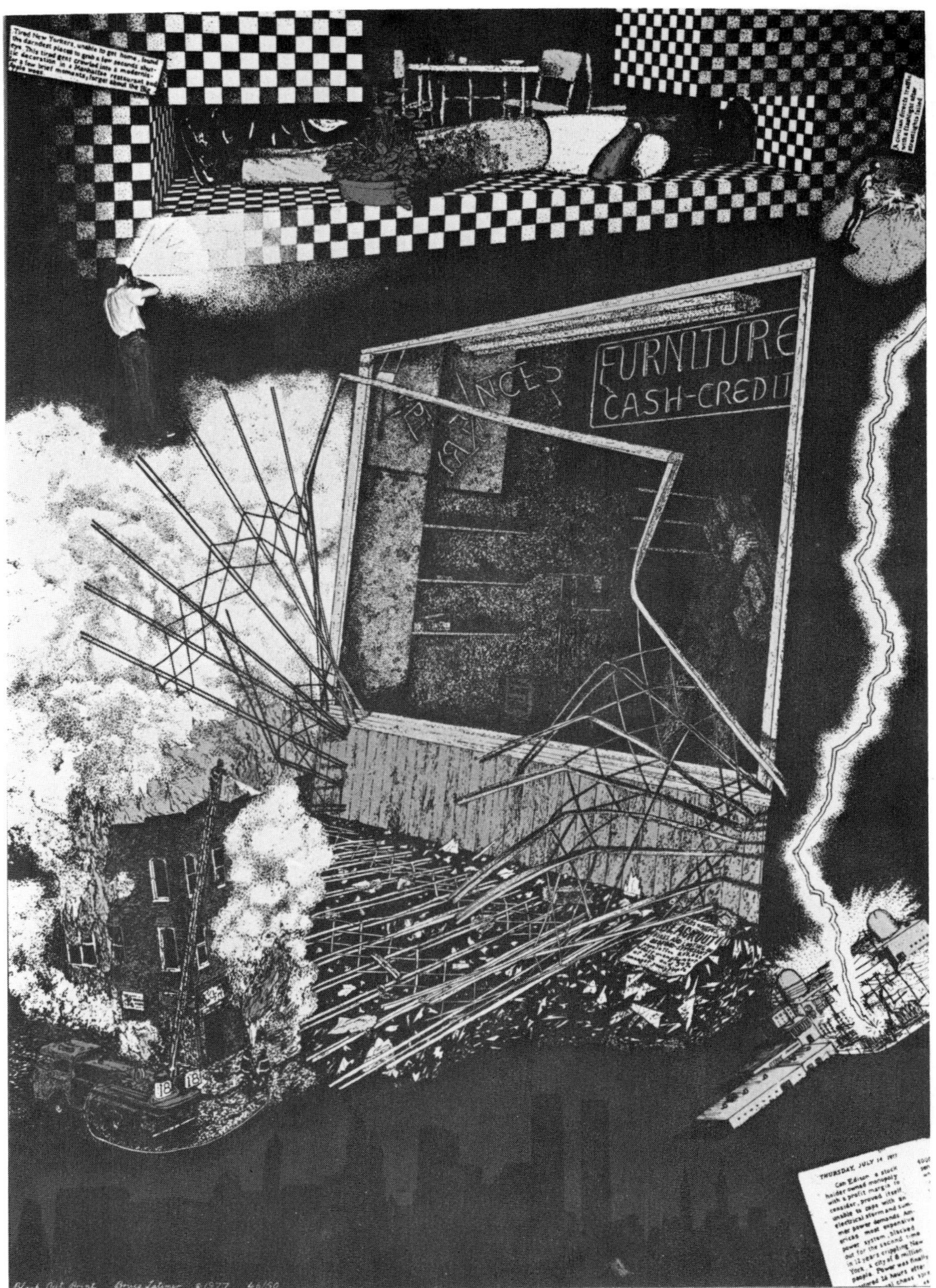

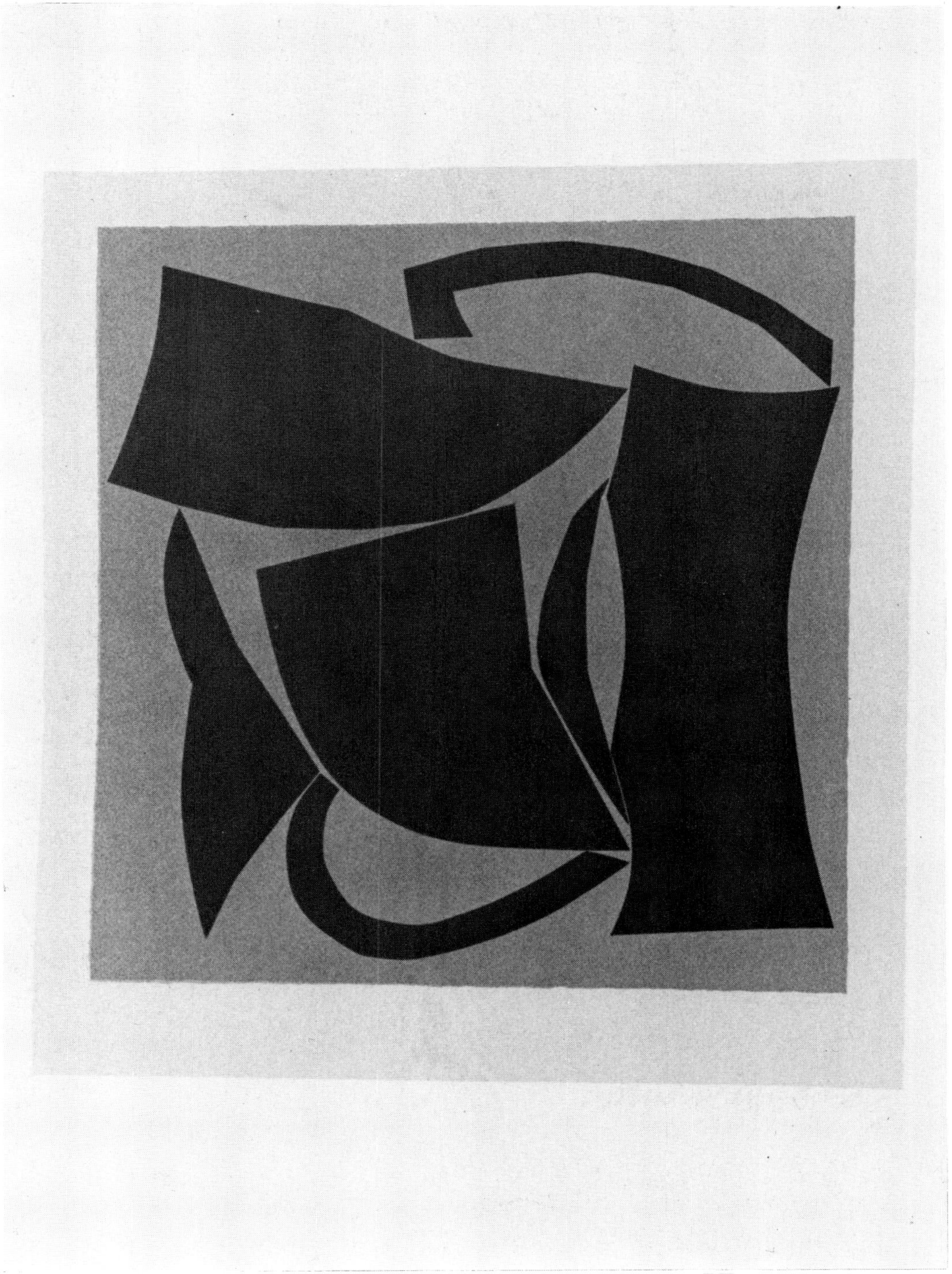

# Alun Leach-Jones

Born United Kingdom 1937; arrived Australia 1960.
Studied Liverpool College of Art, UK 1959-60;
South Australian School of Art 1960-63.
Has held 19 one-man shows Australia, New Zealand,
Malaysia, India.
Participated group exhibitions Australia, UK, Europe,
Japan, SE-Asia, New Zealand, USA.
Represented: Australian National Gallery (ACT); State
and regional galleries; educational institutions; Museum
of Modern Art (New York); National Museum of Wales
(UK); National Art Gallery of Malaysia.
PCA Patron Print edition commissioned 1967.
Lives and works Sydney, NSW.

33 *From the Voyager Suite — Blue and Yellow*
   Screenprint      Moelen de Gue
   45 x 44 cm       Ed. 30

34 *From the Voyager Suite — Blue*
   Screenprint      Moelen de Gue
   45 x 44 cm       Ed. 30

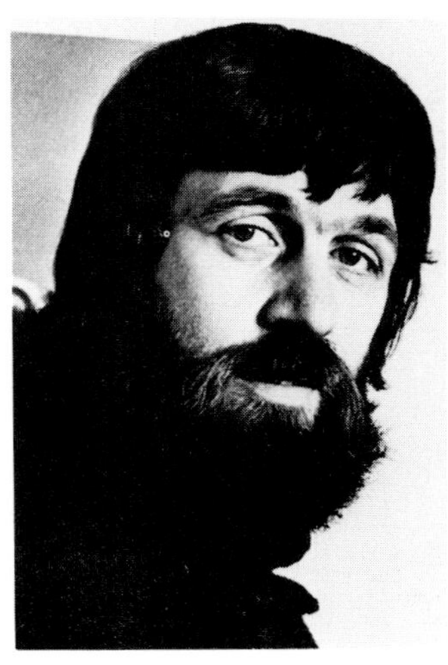

# Bea Maddock



Born Tasmania 1934.
Studied Hobart Technical College 1952-56;
Slade School, London 1959-61.
Has held 20 one-man shows Australia.
Participated group exhibitions Australia; Australian
Prints Today (USA 1966); Images (India 1972);
International Print Biennale (Yugoslavia 1971 '75 '77);
Pratt Graphics Centre (USA 1972); International Print
Biennale (Poland 1972 '74 '76); Australian Prints (UK
1972); Figura 2 (East Germany 1977); Commonwealth
Print Portfolio (Canada 1978).
Represented: Australian National Gallery (ACT); State
and regional galleries; educational institutions;
Museum of Modern Art (New York).
PCA Member Print edition commissioned 1974.
Lectures The Victorian College of the Arts.

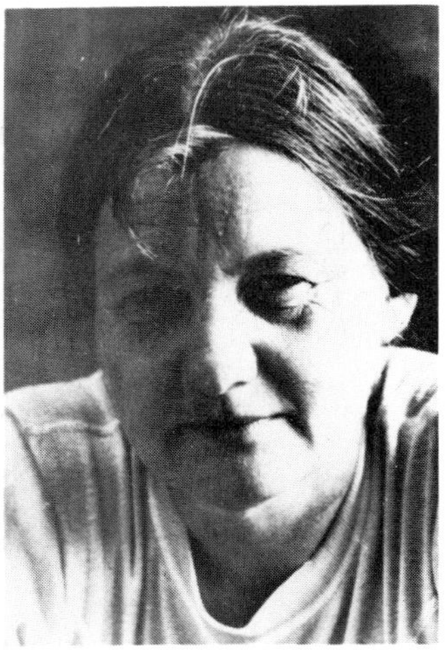

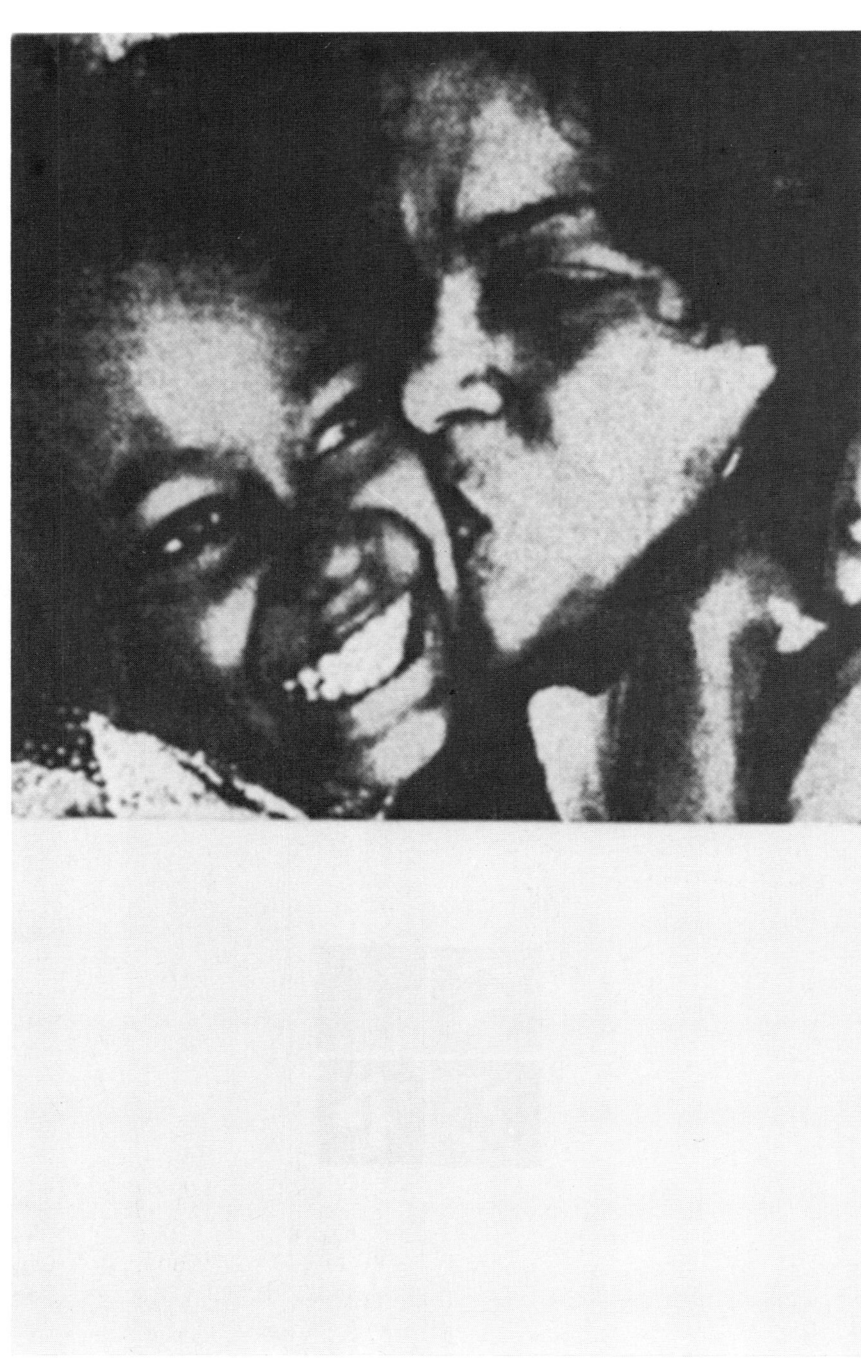

35  *Four By Two I*
    Etching          Rives Velin Cuve
    43 x 30 cm     Ed. 10

36  *Four By Two IV*
    Etching          Rives Velin Cuve
    40 x 31 cm     Ed. 10

# Allan Mitelman

Born Poland 1946; arrived Australia 1953.
Studied Prahran College of Advanced Education,
Melbourne 1965-68.
Has held 12 one-man shows Australia.
Participated group exhibitions Australia; international
print biennials (Japan, Poland); Australian Imprint (SE-
Asia 1971); Images (India 1972); Australian Prints (UK
1972); Australian Graphics (South America 1974); 1st
Western Pacific Print Biennale 1976.
Represented: Australian National Gallery (ACT); State
and regional galleries; educational institutions;
Museum of Modern Art (New York).
PCA Member Print edition commissioned 1971.
Lectures The Victorian College of the Arts.

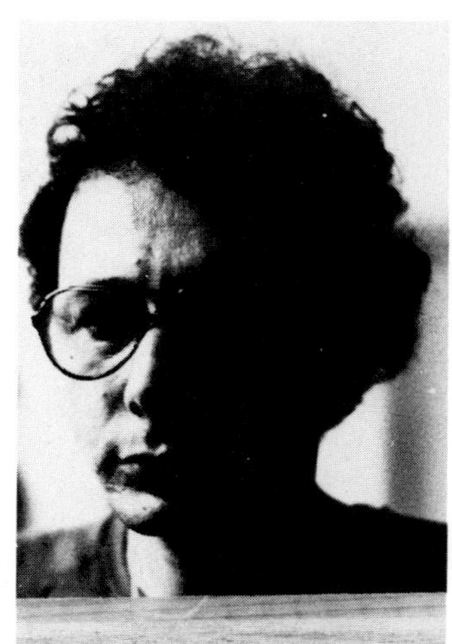

37 *Perdido*
   Etching          Arches
   22 x 28 cm       Ed. 20

38 *Naguine*
   Etching          Arches
   22 x 28 cm       Ed. 20

# Greg Moncrieff

Born Melbourne 1950.
Studied Royal Melbourne Institute of Technology 1969-73.
Has held 3 one-man shows Australia.
Participated group exhibitions Australia;
5th International Print Biennale (Poland 1974);
1st Western Pacific Print Biennale 1976;
PCA Exhibition (Japan, Fiji 1977).
Represented: Australian National Gallery (ACT); regional galleries; educational institutions.
PCA Member Print edition commissioned 1972.
Lectures Melbourne State College, Vic.

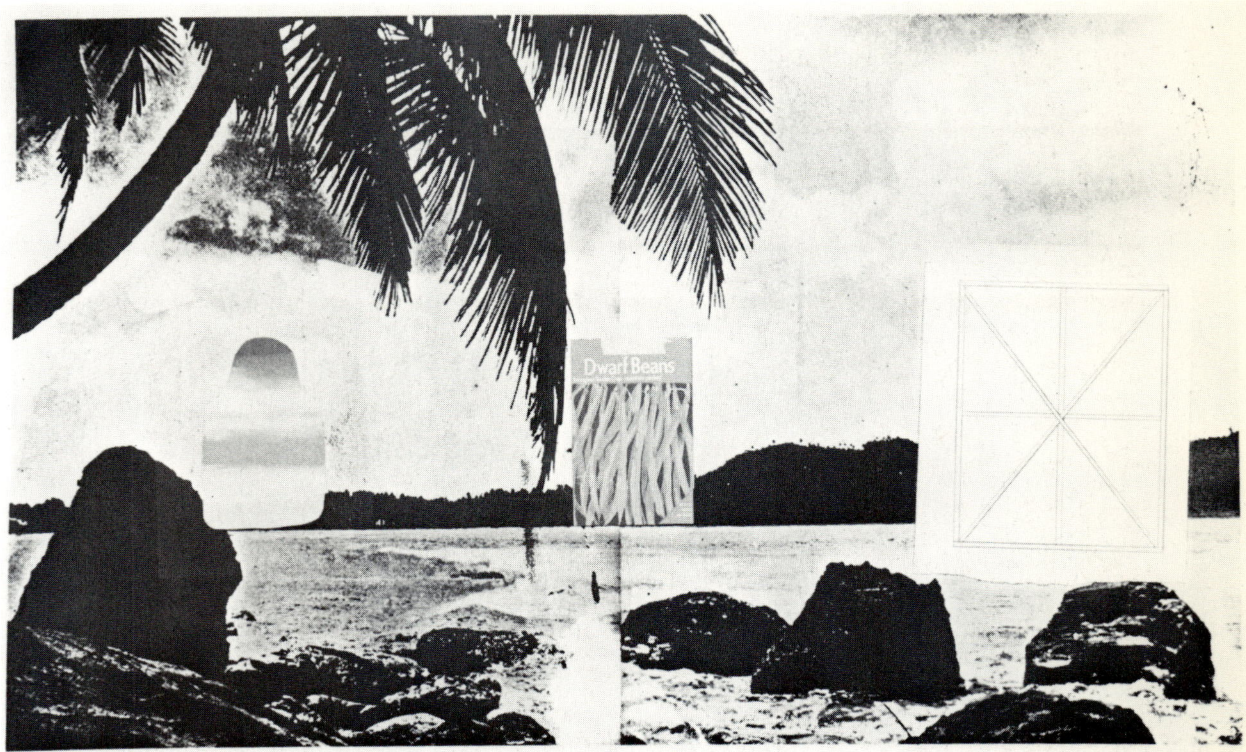


40

39  *Scene From A Lovers Past*
    Screenprint     BFK Rives
    69 x 89 cm      Ed. 18

40  *Tahiti — Not What It Used To Be*
    Screenprint     Greens
    59 x 100 cm     Ed. 12

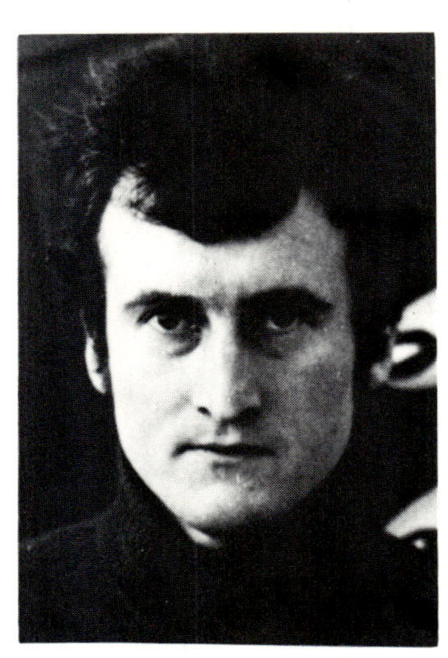

# John Neeson



Born Melbourne 1948.
Studied Royal Melbourne Institute of Technology 1967-69, 1972.
Has held 2 one-man shows Australia.
Participated group exhibitions Australia; Images (India 1972); Pratt Institute (USA 1972); International Print Biennale (Poland 1972); World Print Exhibition (USA 1973); 2nd Western Pacific Print Biennale 1978.
Represented: Australian National Gallery (ACT); State Galleries; Auckland City Art Gallery (New Zealand); Museum of Modern Art (New York).
Lectures Caulfield Institute of Technology, Vic.

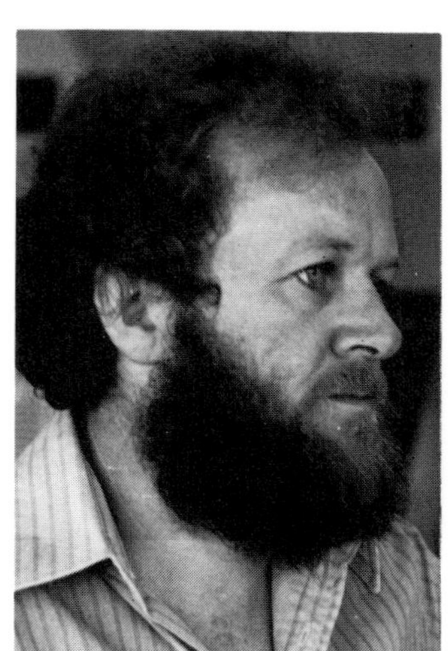

41  *Sometime Ago I Had A Dream; It Was Happy; It Was Laughing*
Etching/aquatint/drypoint    Arches Rives
51 x 66 cm    Ed. 25

42  *Dancing With Mr.*
Etching/aquatint/drypoint    Arches Rives
51 x 102 cm    Ed. 25

# Ann Newmarch

Born South Australia 1945.
Studied Teachers College, South Australia.
Has held one-man shows Australia.
Participated group exhibitions Australia.
Represented: State Gallery (SA).
PCA Member Print edition commissioned 1977.
Lectures Adelaide College of the Arts and Education,
South Australia.

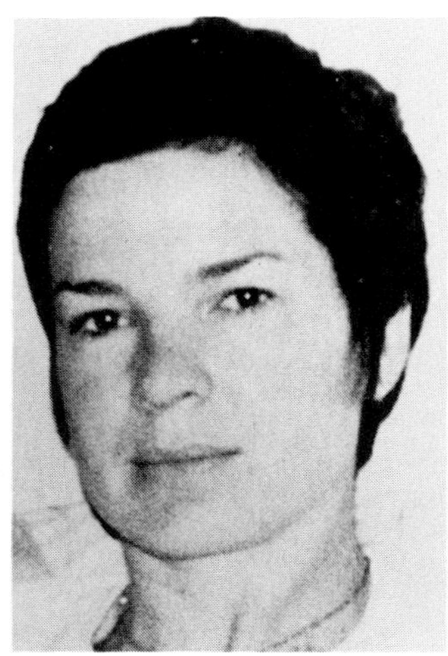

43 *Jake And Bruno 5 yrs & 5 days*
   Screenprint     Arches Dessin
   48 x 71 cm      Ed. 40

44 *Peggy*
   Screenprint     Arches Dessin
   61 x 46 cm      Ed. 20

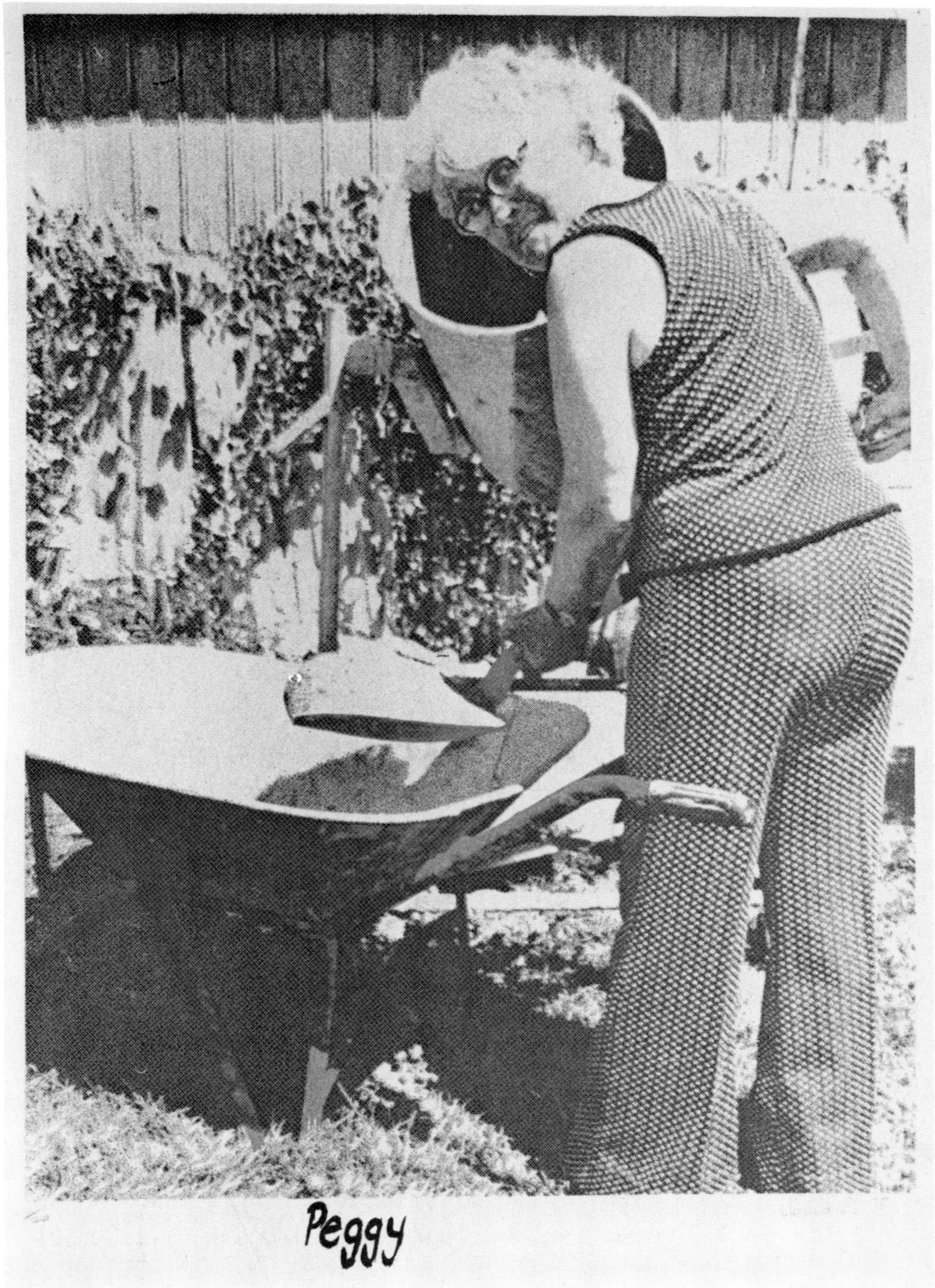

# Graeme Peebles

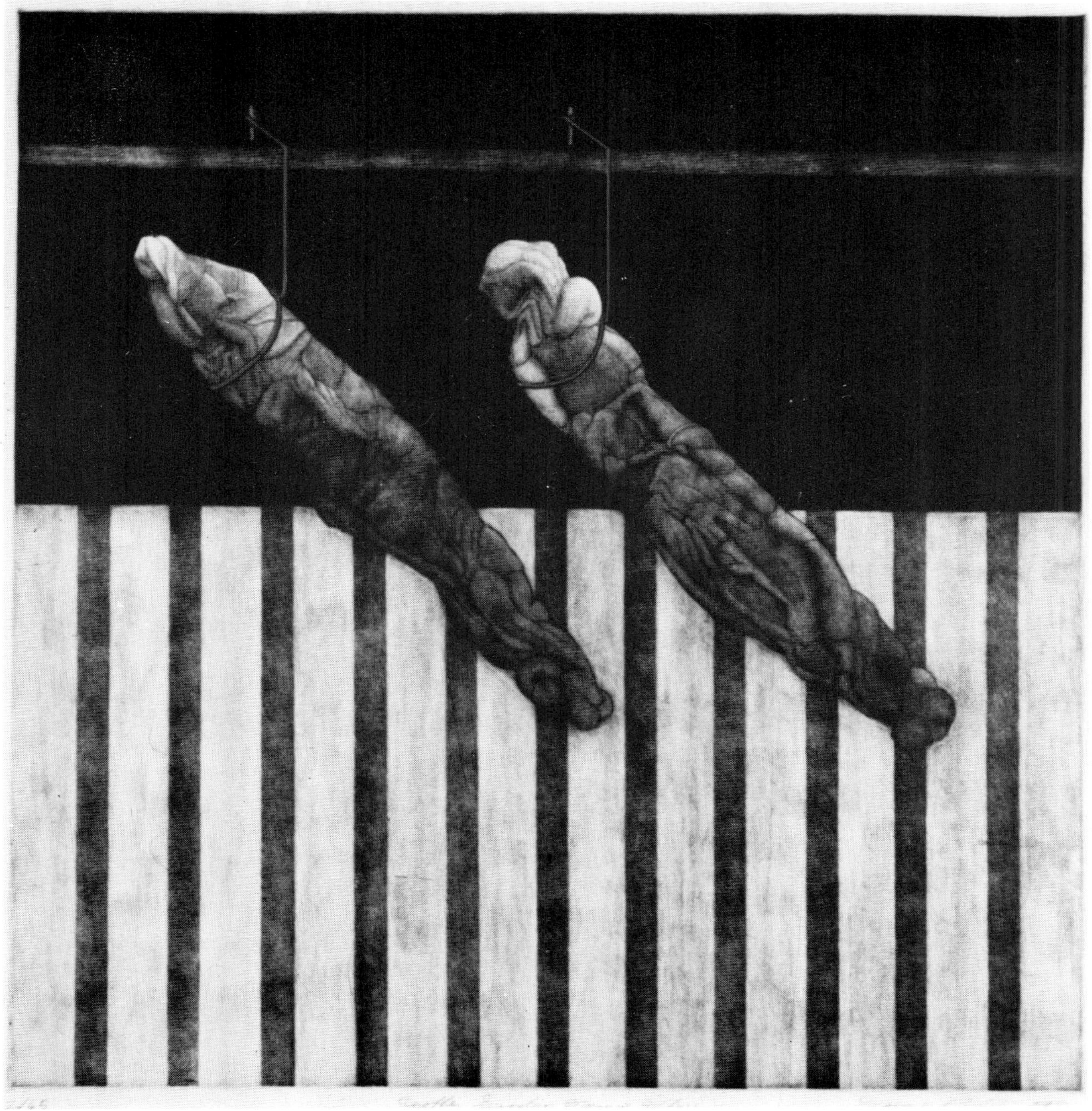

Born Melbourne 1955.
Studied Royal Melbourne Institute of Technology 1973-75.
Participated group exhibitions Australia; PCA Student Exchange Exhibition (UK 1975); 2nd Western Pacific Print Biennale 1978.
PCA Member Print edition commissioned 1979.
Lectures Royal Melbourne Institute of Technology, Vic.

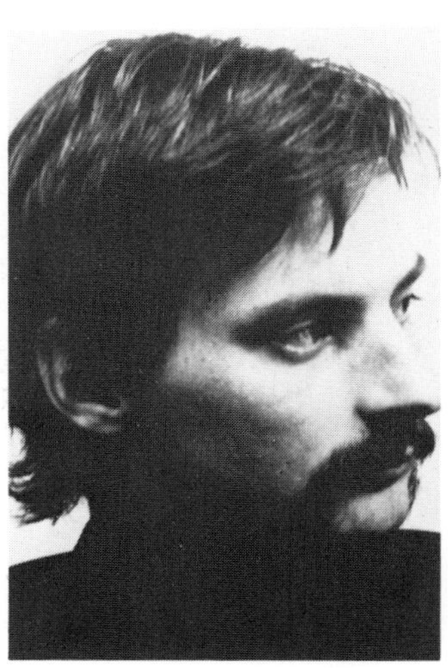

45  *Another Sunday Morning Whore*
Mezzotint      BFK Rives
44 x 44 cm     Ed. 45

46  *Schaedenfreude*
Mezzotint      BFK Rives
50 x 50 cm     Ed. 50

# John Robinson

Born Melbourne 1940.
Studied Royal Melbourne Institute of Technology.
Has held 2 one-man shows Australia.
Participated group exhibitions Australia; PCA Exhibition
(Japan, Fiji 1977); World Print Competition (USA,
Canada 1977); 2nd Western Pacific Print Biennale 1978.
PCA Member Print edition commissioned 1978.
Lives and works Melbourne, Vic.

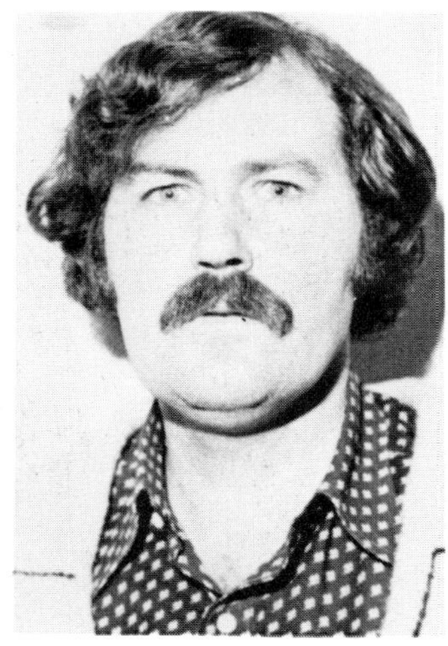

47 *Estoril*
   Lithograph      Arches Velin
   115 x 80 cm    Ed. 15

48 *Rome*
   Lithograph      Arches Velin
   95 x 71 cm     Ed. 11

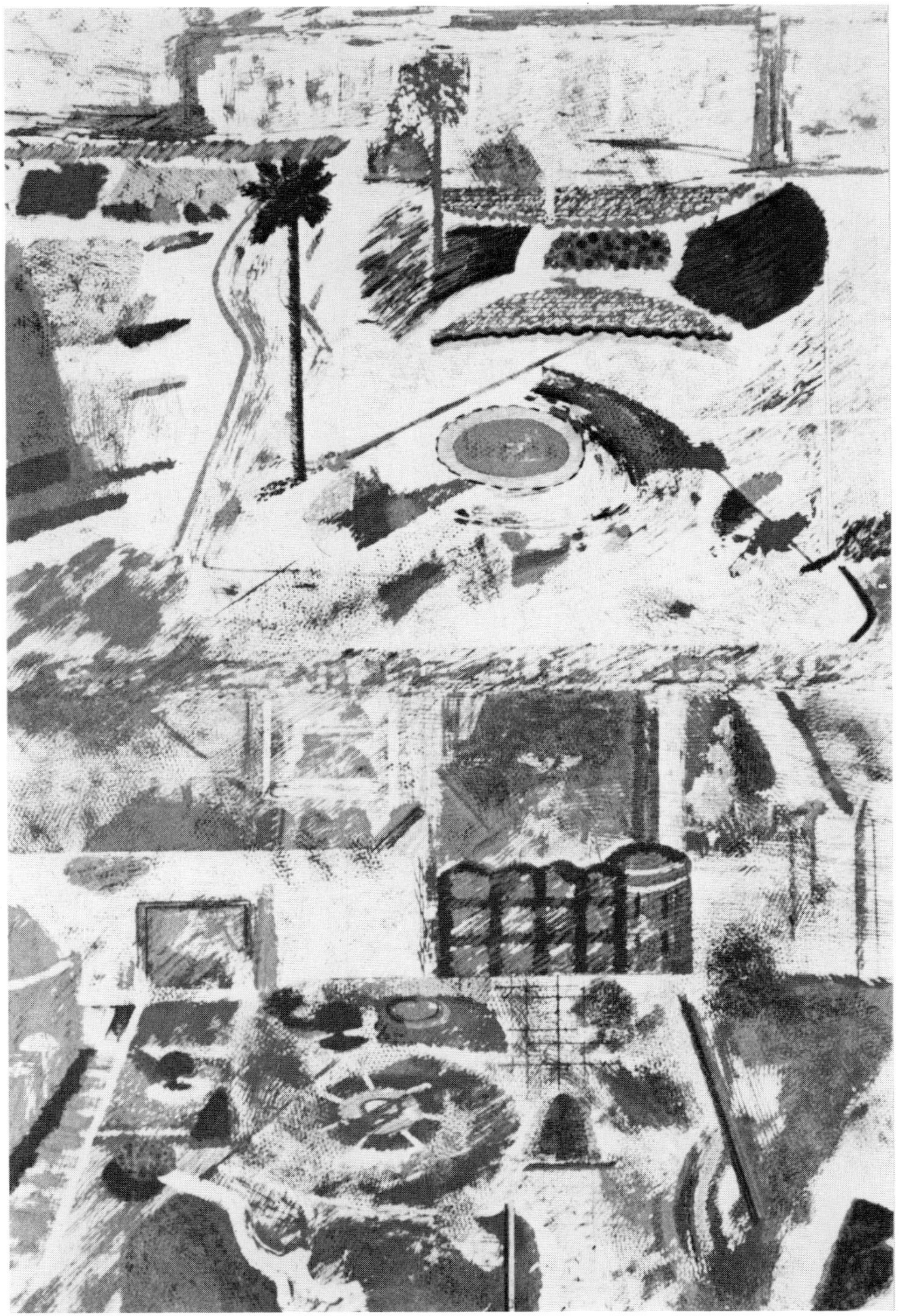

# Sally Robinson



Born England 1952.
Studied National Art School, Sydney 1970-73.
Has held 3 one-man shows Australia.
Participated group exhibitions Australia.
Represented: Australian National Gallery (ACT);
State and regional galleries; educational institutions.
PCA Member Print edition commissioned 1975.
Lives and works Sydney, NSW.

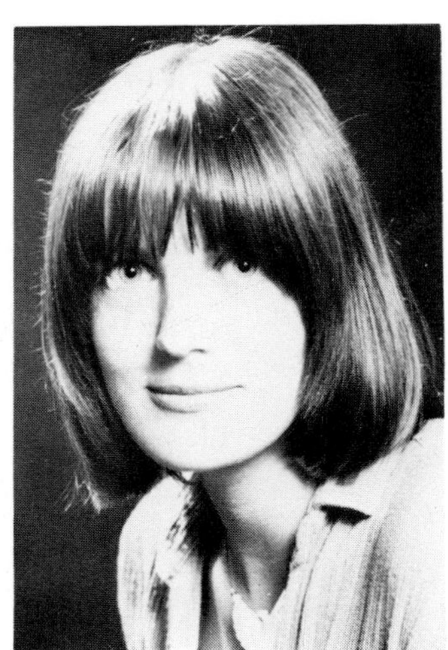

49 *Central Australia*
   Screenprint    Westvaco Inverboard
   80 x 105 cm    Ed. 20

50 *Summer Self Portrait*
   Screenprint    Westvaco Inverboard
   77 x 102 cm    Ed. 25

# David Rose



Born Melbourne 1936.
Studied Escuela Lonja (Spain 1964).
Has held one-man shows Australia.
Participated group exhibitions Australia; Victoria and
Albert Museum (UK 1972); international print biennials
(Italy 1969; UK 1970; Yugoslavia 1972 '74; Poland 1972
'74; Norway 1974; Germany 1974; Spain 1974).
Represented: Australian National Gallery (ACT); State
and regional galleries; Museum of Modern Art (New York).
PCA Member Print edition commissioned 1972.
Lives and works New South Wales.

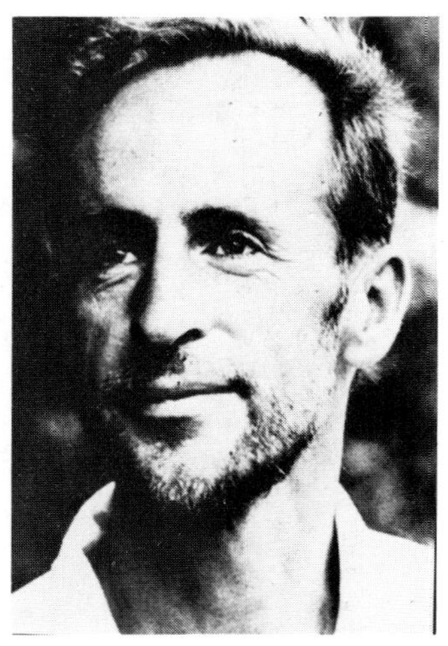

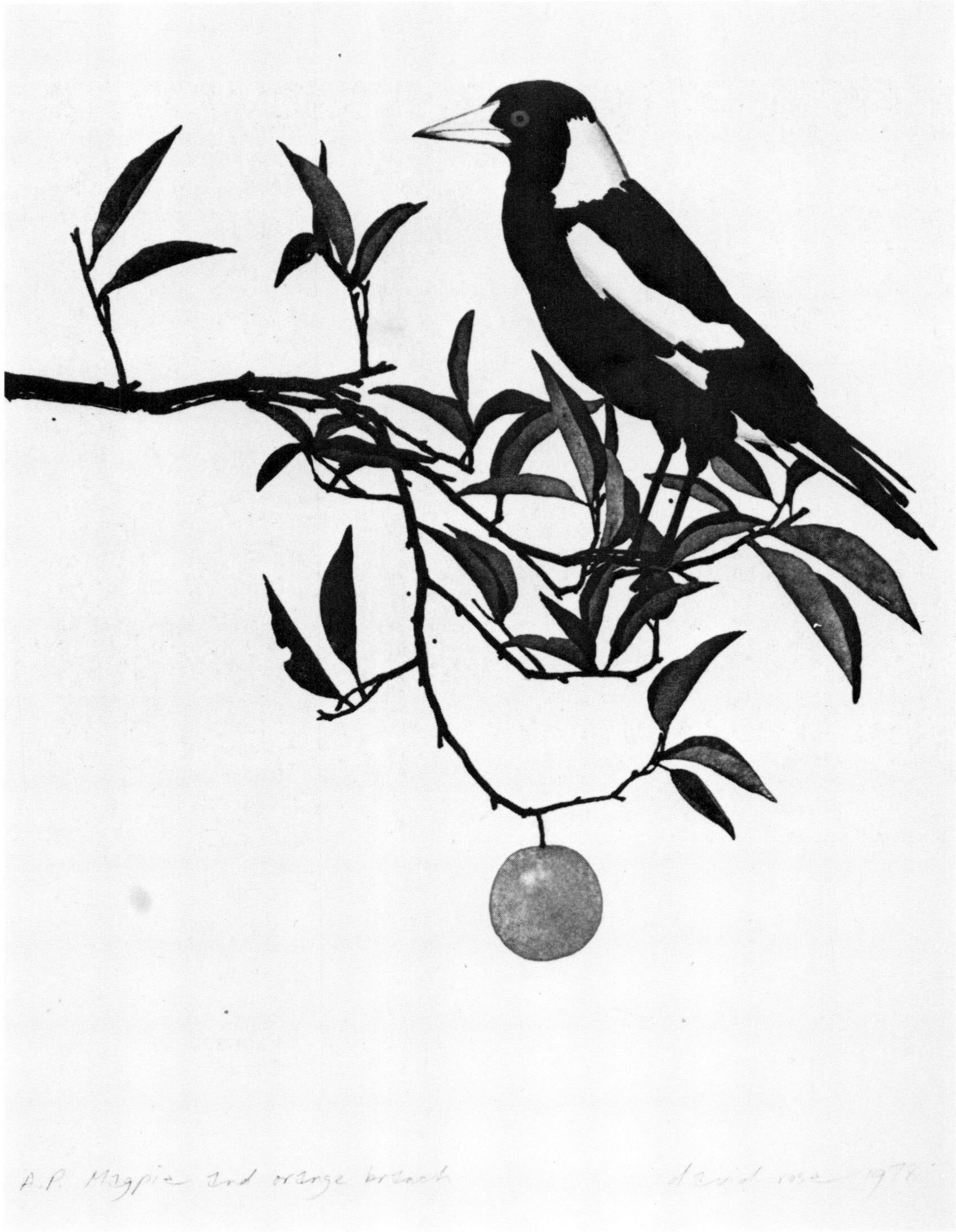

51  *Visiting Spinebill*
    Etching          Rives
    61 x 45 cm      Ed. 50

52  *Magpie And Orange Branch*
    Etching          Arches Velin
    61 x 45 cm      Ed. 50

# Jan Senbergs

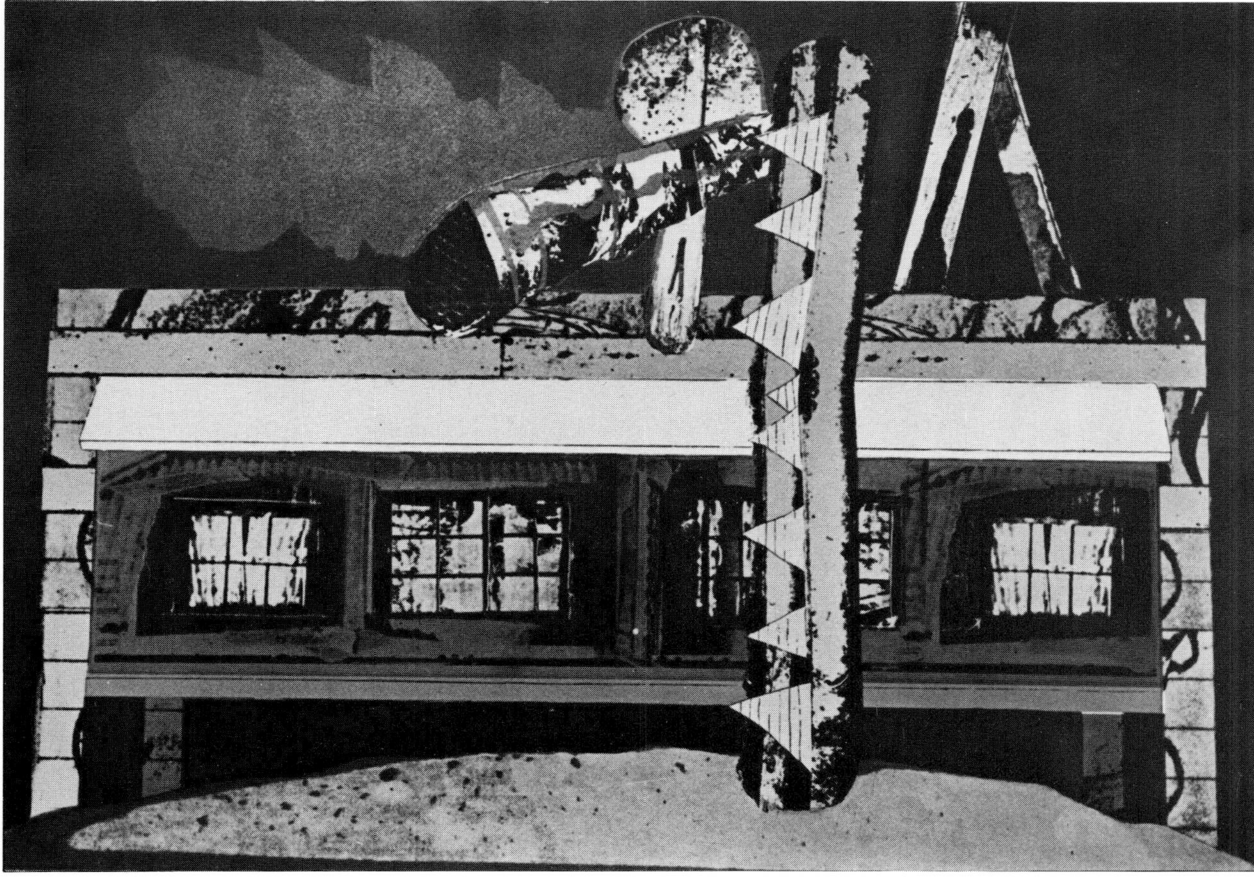



Born Latvia 1939; arrived Australia 1950.
Studied Melbourne School of Printing 1956-59.
Has held 17 one-man shows Australia.
Participated group exhibitions Australia; international
print biennials (Yugoslavia, Poland, Japan, UK); 10th &
12th International Biennale of Modern Art (South
America 1969 '73); Australian Prints (UK 1972); PCA
Exhibition (Japan, Fiji 1977).
Represented: Australian National Gallery (ACT); State
and regional galleries; Museum of Modern Art (New York).
PCA Patron Print edition commissioned 1977.
Lives and works Melbourne, Vic.

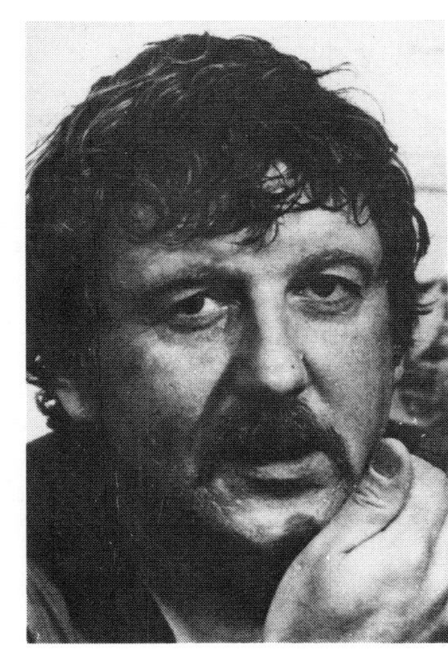

53  *The Good Looking Print, Or Harry Was Right*
   Screenprint    Fabriano
   56 x 81 cm    Ed. 17

54  *A Vision For Builders*
   Screenprint    Fabriano
   55 x 81 cm    Ed. 24

# Stephen Spurrier

Born Melbourne 1946.
Studied Royal Melbourne Institute of Technology 1967-70.
Has held 6 one-man shows Australia.
Participated group exhibitions Australia; Bradford Print
Biennale (UK 1968 '70); Pratt Graphics Centre (USA
1974); 2nd Western Pacific Print Biennale 1978.
Represented: Australian National Gallery (ACT); State
and regional galleries; educational institutions, Museum
of Modern Art (New York).
Lectures Melbourne State College, Vic.

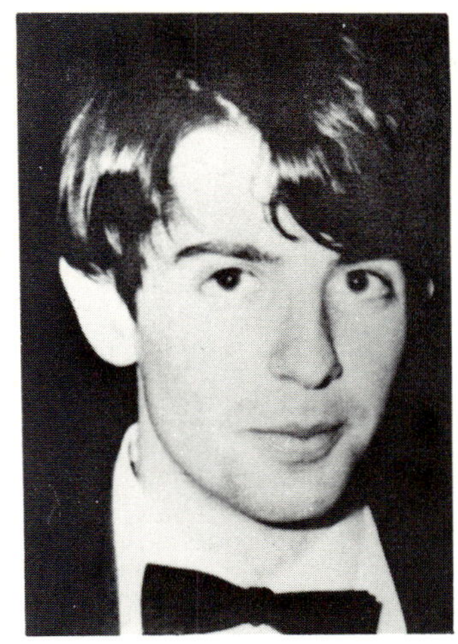

55 *Arbolista*
   Etching          Arches Velin Rives
   15 x 50 cm        Ed. 10

56 *Forego*
   Etching          Arches Velin Rives
   23 x 52 cm        Ed. 20

55

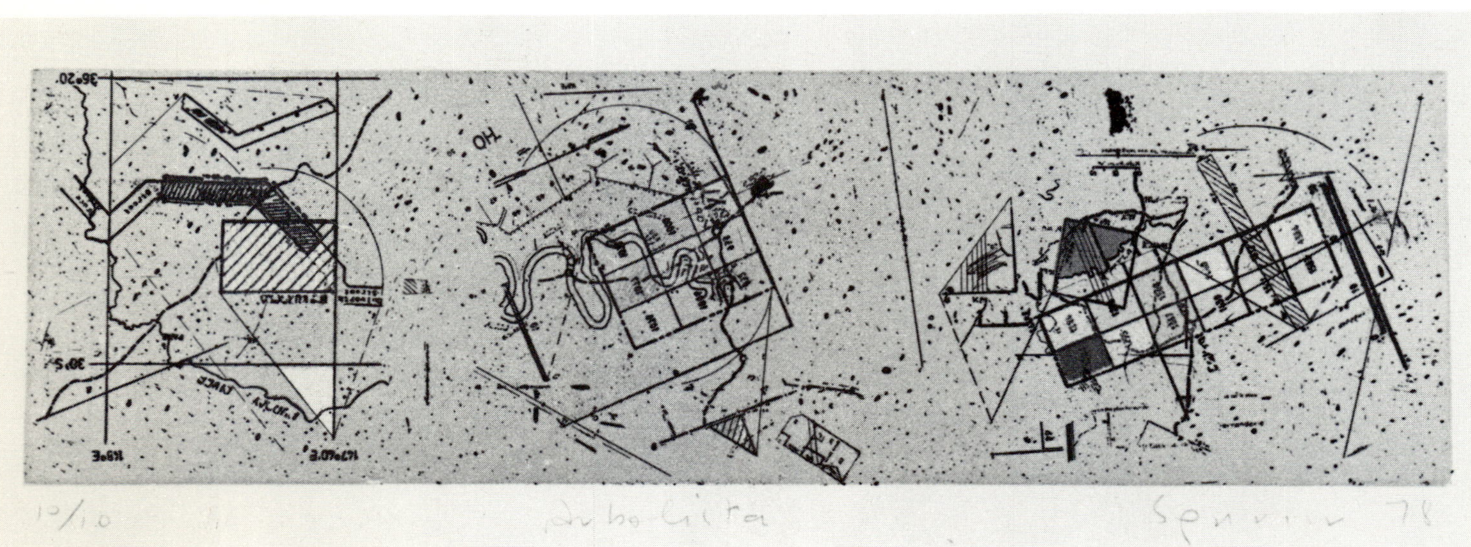

# Tim Storrier

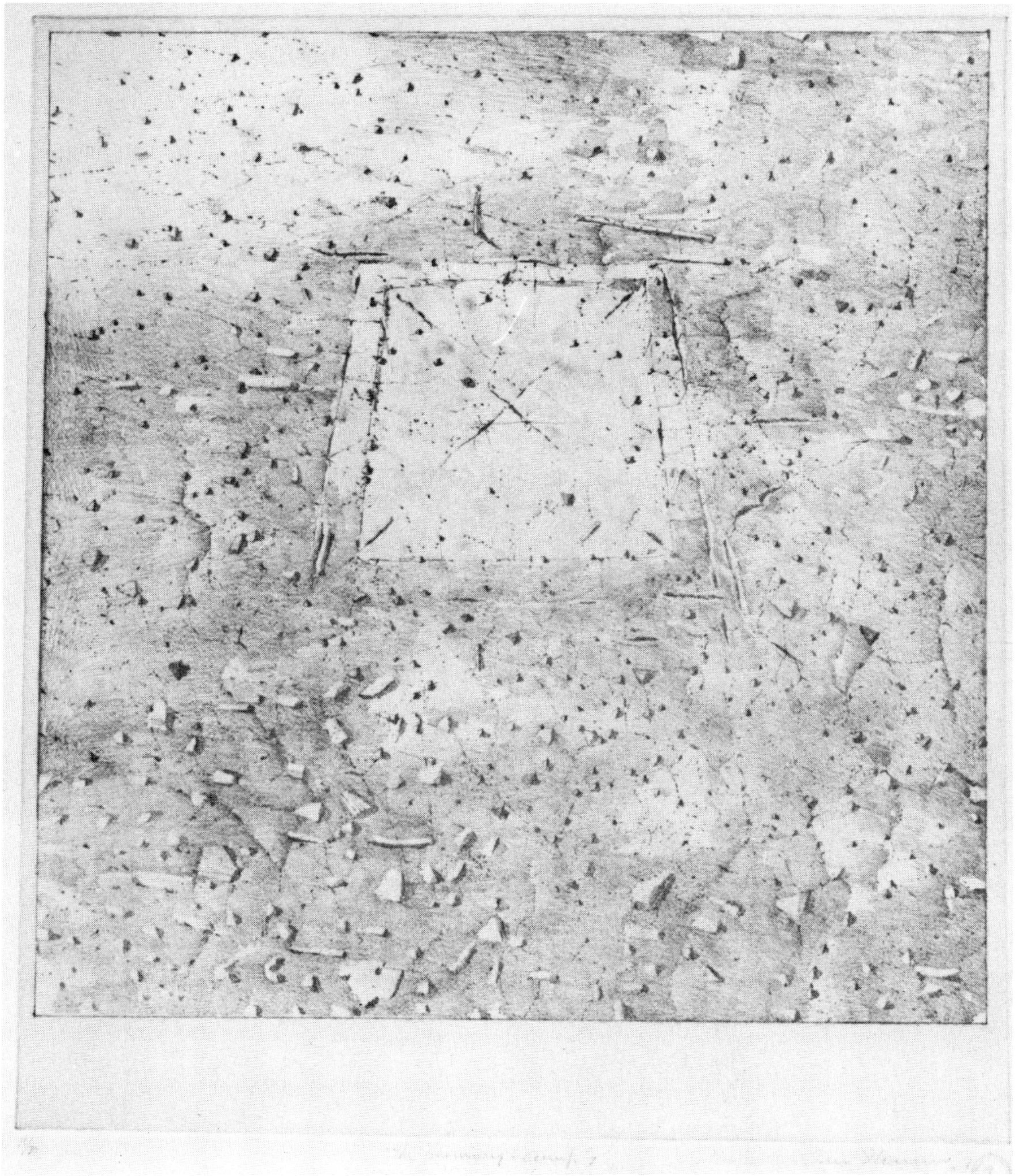

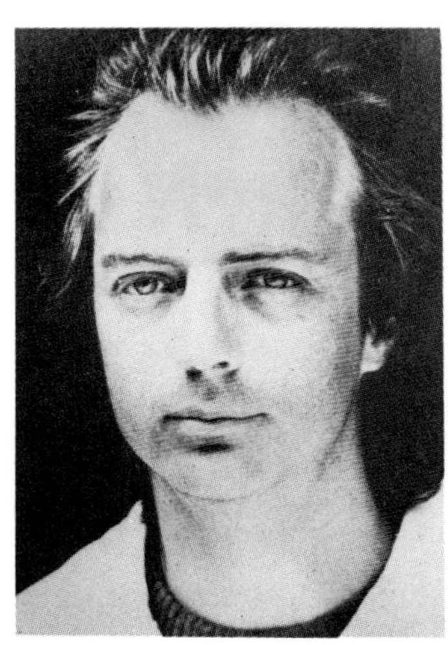

Born Sydney 1949.
Studied National Art School, Sydney 1967-69.
Has held 8 one-man shows Australia.
Participated group exhibitions Australia.
Lives and works Sydney, NSW.

57  *The Flag, Camp At Relay*
Screenprint/collage
50 x 53 cm      Ed. 75

58  *The Memory, Sunup 7*
Etching
51 x 45 cm      Ed. 70

Courtesy Holdsworth Galleries NSW

# Helen Taylor

Born India; arrived Australia 1952.
Studied Claremont Technical College (WA) 1972.
Held one-man show Australia 1978.
Participated group exhibitions Australia; PCA Exhibition (Japan, Fiji 1977); 2nd Western Pacific Print Biennale 1978.
Represented: Australian National Gallery (ACT); State Gallery (WA); educational institutions.
PCA Member Print edition commissioned 1978.
Lives and works Perth, WA.

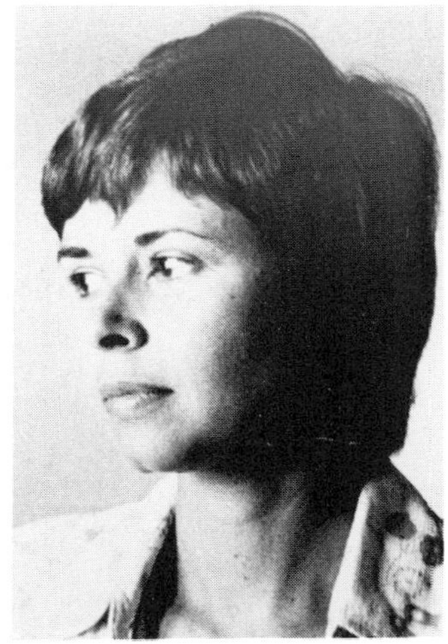

59 *Paulines' Outside*
   Etching        BFK Rives
   63 x 50 cm     Ed. 20

60 *Dresser*
   Etching        Murillo
   45 x 31 cm     Ed. 20



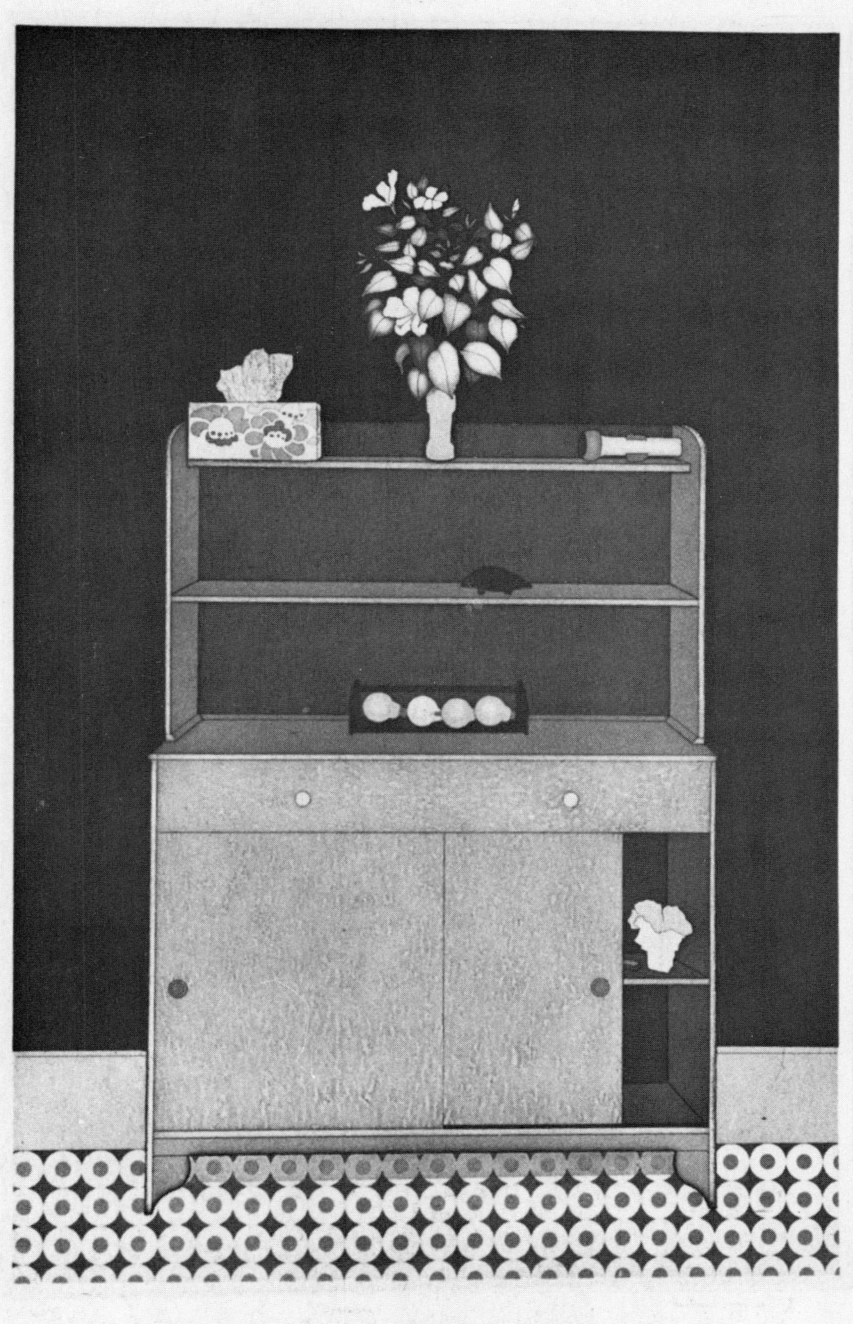

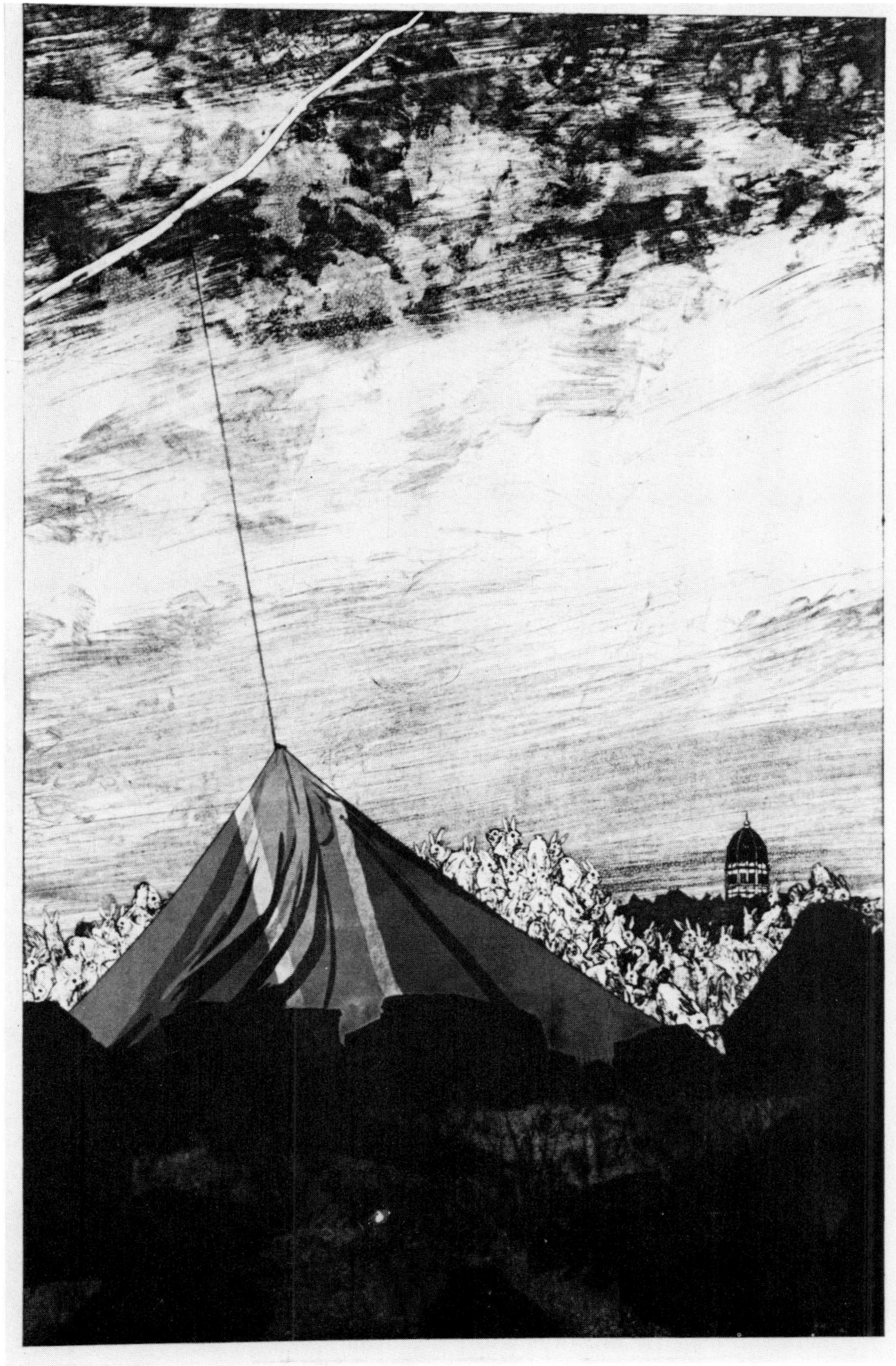

# James Taylor

Born Melbourne 1941.
Studied Caulfield Institute of Technology, Melbourne;
Royal Melbourne Institute of Technology.
Has held 2 one-man shows Australia.
Participated group exhibitions Australia; International
Print Biennale (Poland 1971 '72); Victoria & Albert
Museum (UK 1972); Images (India 1972); Pratt
Graphics Centre (USA 1973); 1st Western Pacific Print
Biennale 1976; PCA Exhibition (Japan, Fiji 1977).
Represented: Australian National Gallery (ACT); State
and regional galleries; educational institutions; MARA
Institute (Malaysia).
PCA Patron Print edition commissioned 1972.
Lectures Melbourne State College, Vic.

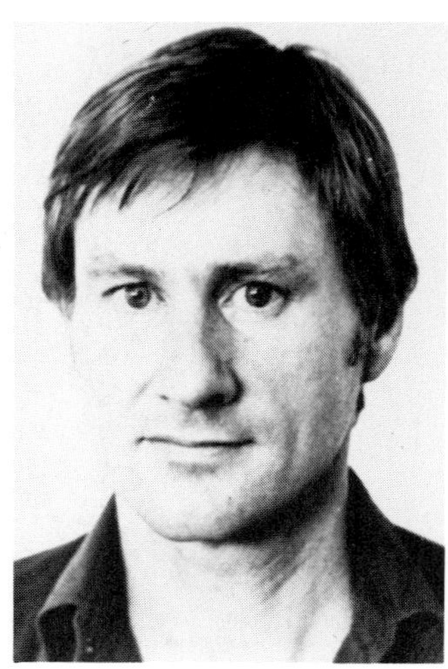

61 *Boolara Campsite*
Etching          Arches
63 x 48 cm     Ed. 10

62 *Colonial Impression*
Etching          Arches
77 x 51 cm     Ed. 10

# Murray Walker



Born Victoria 1937.
Studied Slade School, London 1960-62.
Has held one-man shows Australia.
Participated group exhibitions Australia; Australian
Prints (USA 1966 '73); PCA Exhibition (Japan, Fiji 1977);
2nd Western Pacific Print Biennale 1978.
Represented: Australian National Gallery (ACT); State
and regional galleries; educational institutions;
Smithsonian Institute (Washington USA).
PCA Member Print edition commissioned 1974.
Lives and works Melbourne, Vic.

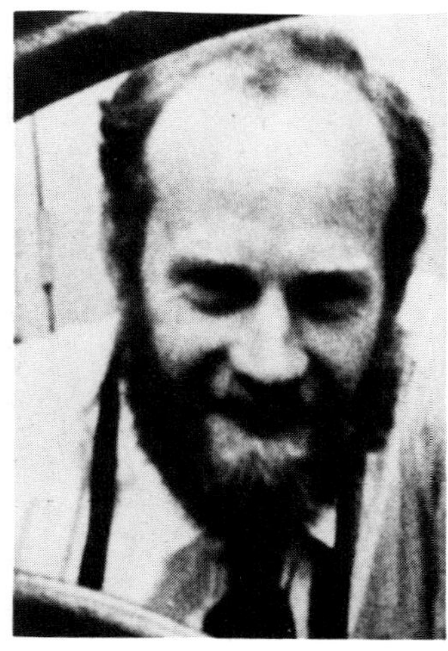

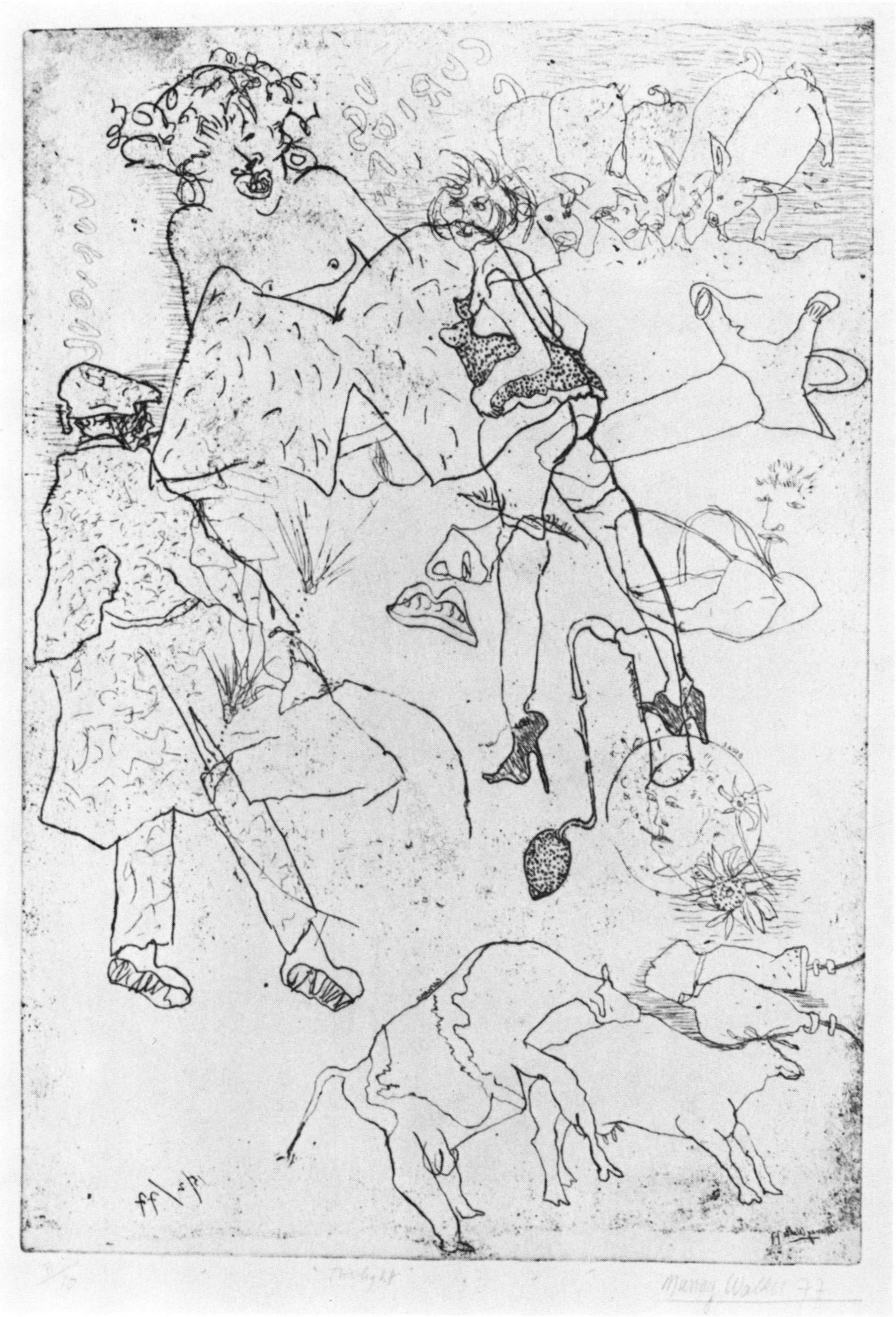

63  *Vignettes Entertainers At Rest*
    Etching          Barcham Green's Hayle Mill
    35 x 51 cm    Ed. 7

64  *Twilight*
    Etching          Barcham Green's Hayle Mill
    51 x 35 cm    Ed. 10

# Arthur Wicks



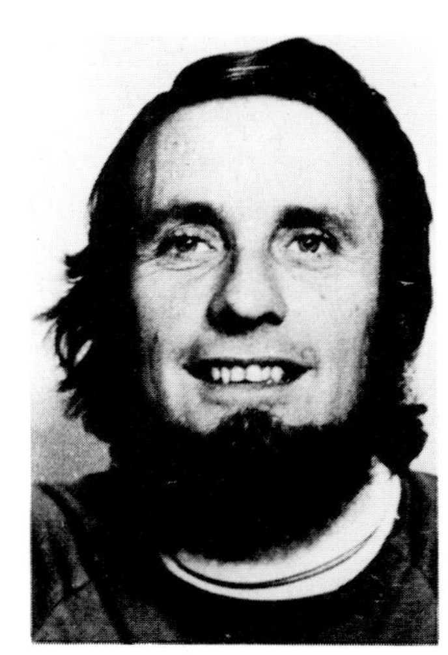

Born Sydney 1937.
Studied Sydney University 1959; Australian National University (ACT) 1964; Hayters Studio 17 (Paris) 1967.
Has held 8 one-man shows Australia, Paris.
Participated group exhibitions Australia; PCA Exhibition (Japan, Fiji 1977); Pratt Graphics Centre (USA 1978); 2nd Western Pacific Print Biennale 1978.
Represented: Australian National Gallery (ACT); State and regional galleries; educational institutions.
PCA Member Print edition commissioned 1978.
Lectures Riverina College of Advanced Education, Wagga Wagga, NSW.

65  *Kit For Grasping The World*
    Screenprint    Arches 88
    68 x 57 cm     Ed. 60

66  *Four Steps — Three Times*
    Screenprint    Saunders
    70 x 93 cm     Ed. 18

# Normana Wight

Born Melbourne 1936.
Studied Royal Melbourne Institute of Technology;
Central School of Art, London; Florence University, Italy.
Has held one-man shows Australia.
Participated group exhibitions Australia; Images (India 1972).
Represented: State and regional galleries; educational institutions.
PCA Member Print edition commissioned 1975.
Lectures Preston Institute of Technology, Melbourne, Vic.

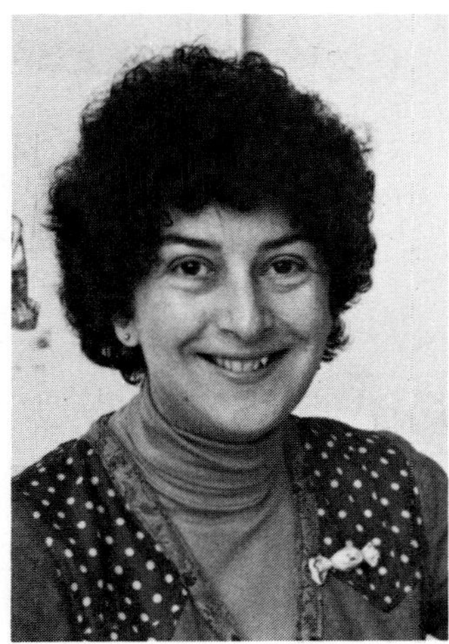

67 *Crochet Jacket*
   Screenprint    Arches 88
   32 x 66 cm    Ed. 12

68 *Ken's Jumper*
   Screenprint    Arches 88
   76 x 40 cm    Ed. 15



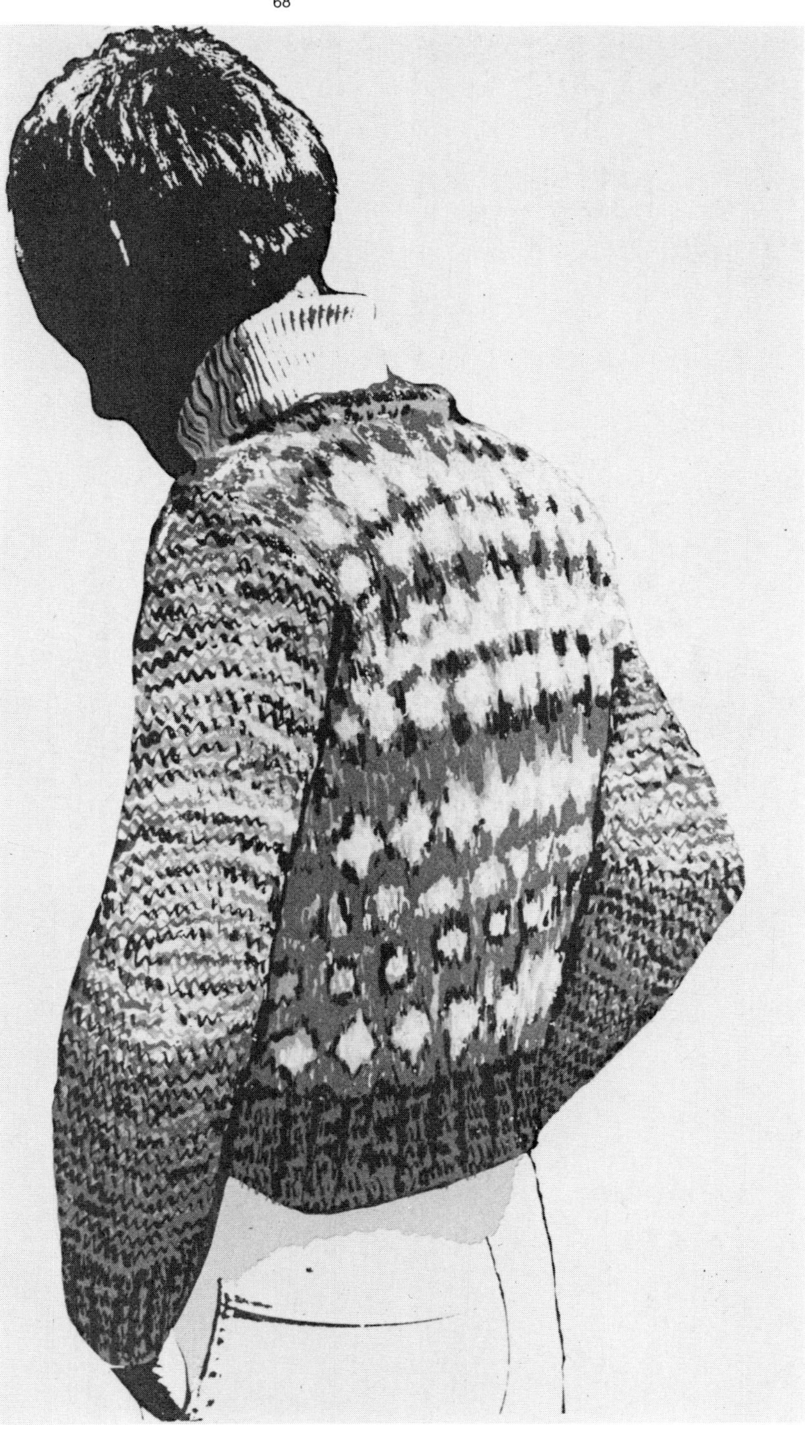

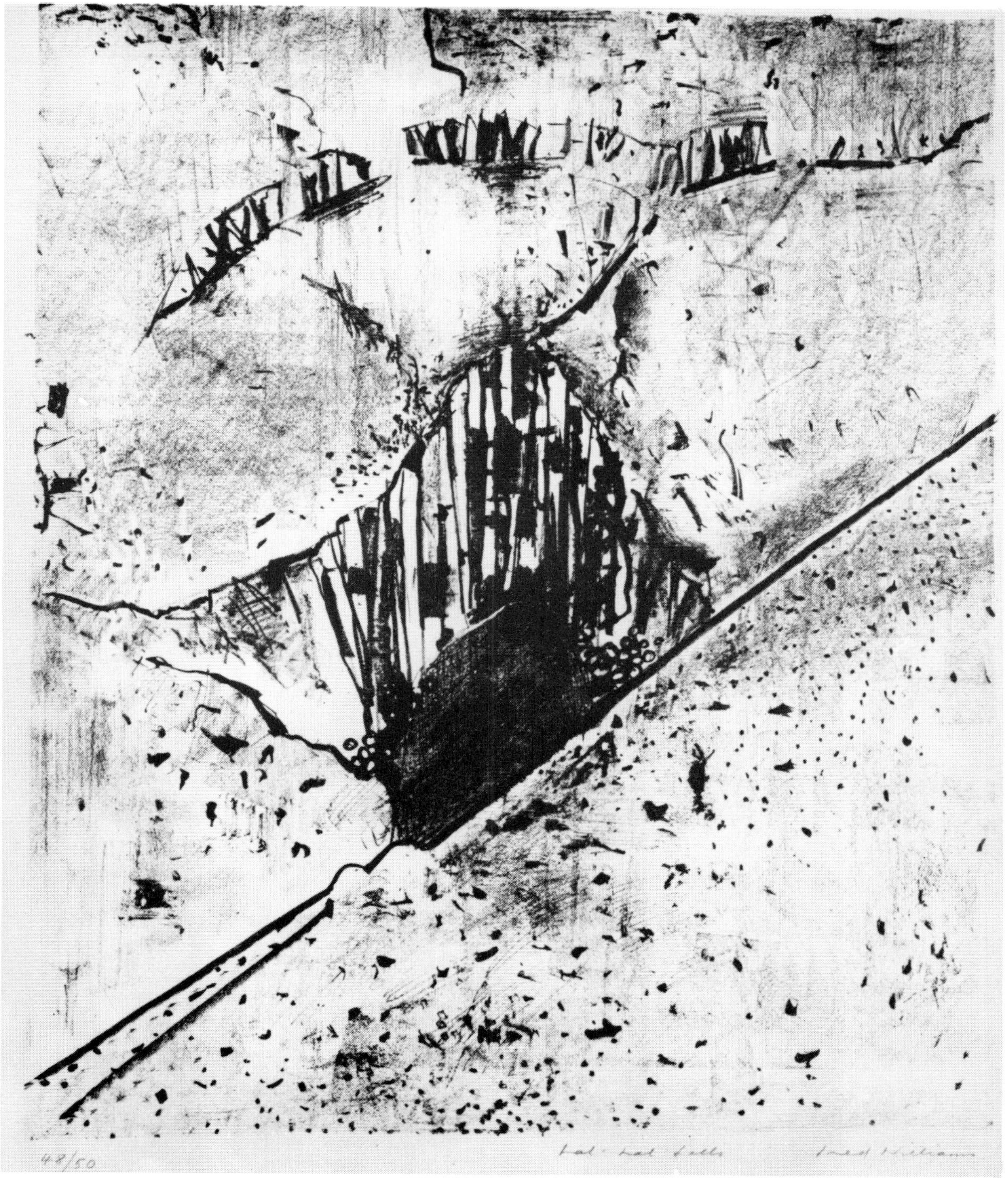

# Fred Williams

Born Melbourne 1927.
Studied National Gallery School, Melbourne 1944-49;
Central School and Chelsea School of Art, London
1950-56.
Has held one-man shows Australia and overseas.
Participated group exhibitions Australia; international
print biennials (Poland, Switzerland, Japan); Images
(India 1972); Australian Prints (USA 1973).
Represented: Australian National Gallery (ACT); State
and regional galleries; Museum of Modern Art (New
York); Victoria & Albert Museum (London).
PCA Patron Print edition commissioned 1968.
Lives and works Melbourne, Vic.

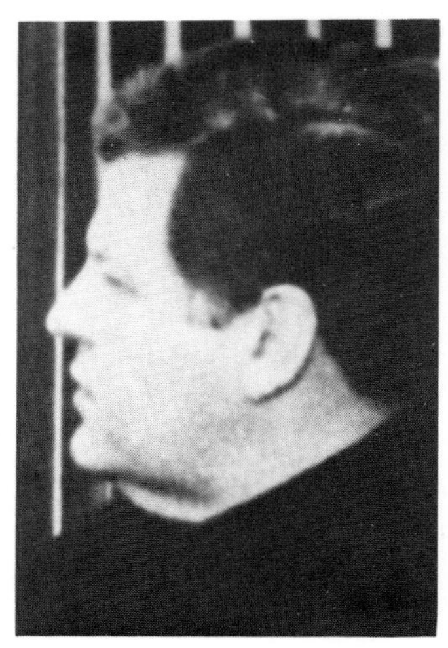

69  *Wild Dog Creek 1*
Lithograph     BFK Rives
62 x 46 cm     Ed. 50

70  *Lal-Lal Falls*
Lithograph     BFK Rives
53 x 46 cm     Ed. 50

# Publications

## Catalogues, Posters 1967-79
Print Prize Exhibitions 1976-8-9
Ten Printmakers 1970
Student Printmakers 1971-2-3
Polish Printmakers 1972
Australian Graphics 1972-3
Print Prize Exhibition 1973
Australian Student Printmakers
Six x Four
Five New Zealand Printmakers
Twelve Australian Lithographers 1975
Contemporary Japanese Prints 1976
1st Western Pacific Print Biennale 1976
Australian Student Printmakers 1977
West Surrey Student Printmakers 1977
Prints and Drawings 1978
Australian Etching 1978
2nd Western Pacific Print Biennale 1978
Print Council of Australia Exhibition 1976-78
Australian Student Printmakers 1979
German Student Printmakers 1979
Contemporary Swedish Prints 1979
Contemporary Australian Printmakers I, 1979

## Books

Directory of Australian Printmakers (ed. Lilian Wood/Lansdowne 1976)
Contemporary Australian Printmakers (Franz Kempf/Lansdowne 1976)


# Imprint 1966—79: articles and essays

**1966**

No. 1 (Original format 22.5 x 14 cm)
Inaugural issue statement — Harley Preston
What is an original print? — Udo Sellbach

**1967**

1 Introduction — Harley Preston
Technique in Printmaking — Udo Sellbach
Membership prints — Udo Sellbach
2 Engraving — Murray Walker
3 Printing possibilities versus medium possibilities — Udo Sellbach

**1968**

1 Lithography — Grahame King
2 Arthur Boyd's St Francis lithographs — Margaret Plant
3 Print collecting — Udo Sellbach

**1969**

1 Bradford Print Biennale
Fred Williams — Etchings (book review) — Udo Sellbach
2 Print Room Collection of the National Gallery of
Victoria — Ursula Hoff
Report of USA, Europe tour — Ruth Faerber
3 Etchings by Baldessin — Margaret Plant
Geneva Centre for Contemporary Gravure — Neil R. Caffin

**1970**

1 Comments on tour, London and New York — Grahame King
2 Noel Counihan — Udo Sellbach
Patron and member prints 1970 (with reproductions)
3 Barnett Newman 1905-1970

**1971**

1 Alois Senefelder 1771-1834
2 Technique of seriograph
Patron and member prints 1971 (with reproductions)
Lecture series: Appreciating original prints
3 Print Council of Australia — 5th year

**1972**

1 Printmaking in Poland (text condensed by Lilian
Wood from original manuscript Contemporary
Polish Graphic Art Piotr Krakowski, Cracow,
November 1971)
2 Patron and member prints 1972 (with reproductions)
3 Taking care of prints — James H. Taylor

**1973**

1 Art Prize syndrome
2 Patron and member prints 1973 (with reproductions)
3 Print Council of Australia Collection 1967-72
(exhibition leaflet)

**1974**

1 Paper and printmaking — Robert Grieve
2 (New format 29 x 20.5 cm — editor
Geoff La Gerche) — Ann Stephens
Bea Maddock — Suzanne Davies
Mornington Peninsula Arts Centre — Alan McCulloch
Birth of a new press — Neil Jeffreys
3 Sir Lionel Lindsay — printmaker — Peter Lindsay
The Brisbane scene — printmaking — Phyllis Woolcock
Joy Hutton — printmaker — Phyllis Woolcock
Patron and member prints 1974 (with reproductions)
Directory of galleries dealing in original prints


**1975**

No. 1 Franz Kempf — David Dolan
Roger Kemp — Elizabeth Cross
2 David Rose
Letter from Perth — Edgar Karabanovs
Marks on original prints
3 Petr Herel — Elizabeth Cross
Zero Print Workshop — Sydney — Rosemary Vickers
4 Fred Williams — Elizabeth Cross
'Occasional Images from a City Chamber'
(George Baldessin) — Sue Davies
Patron and member prints 1975 (with reproductions)

**1976**

1 Alun Leach-Jones — Janine Burke
Contemporary Japanese prints — Elizabeth Cross
2 Artists As Printmakers — Gary Catalano
Margaret Preston — Janine Burke
3 Noel Counihan — Charles Merewether
Earle Backen — Ruth Faerber
Patron and member prints 1976 (with reproductions)

**1977**

1 Ray Beattie — Craig Gough
Some linocuts by Robin Wallace-Crabbe — Gary Catalano
2 Allan Mitelman — Suzanne Davies
Directory of prizes, bequests and Scholarships in
Australia
3 50 Years of Australian Etching 1890-1940 — Ron Nott
Patron and member prints (with reproductions)
4 Mary Macqueen: Lithographer — Elizabeth Cross
Thea Proctor — Janine Burke

**1978**

(Editor Elizabeth Cross)
1 Political Postering in Australia — Julie Ewington
The Print Collection of the Art Gallery of
South Australia — Alison Carroll
2 A Survey of Australian Relief Prints 1900-1950 — Janine Burke
A directory of galleries dealing in original prints
3 Barbara Hanrahan: A self portrait
Introduction by Alison Carroll
Health Hazards in Printmaking — Michael McCann
Patron and member prints 1978 (with reproductions)

**1979**

1 Christopher Croft — Elizabeth Cross
Letter to the Editor — Wood Engravings of
Edith Trethowan — Hendrik Kolenberg
Addendum to Health Hazards in Printmaking
(previous issue) — Michael McCann
(Editor Alison Fraser)
2 Tate Adams and Melbourne Printmaking — Janine Burke
— Suzanne Davies
— Alison Fraser
Australian Student Printmakers 1979 — Lilian Wood

The Business in the Arts Awards (results)
Handmade Ink : A Primer of Basic Principles — Virginia A Myers